WHAT DO
WOMEN
WANT FROM
MEN?

Dan True is a former TV weatherman and pilot for news crews. Now a writer living in Albuquerque, New Mexico, he also enjoys public-speaking. He has previously written *Hummingbirds of North America, A Family of Eagles* and *Flying Free*.

WHAT DO WOMEN WANT FROM MEN?

DAN TRUE
WITH ONE HUNDRED WOMEN

RUPA

Published by
Rupa Publications India Pvt. Ltd 2013
7/16, Ansari Road, Daryaganj
New Delhi 110002

Sales centres:
Allahabad Bengaluru Chennai
Hyderabad Jaipur Kathmandu
Kolkata Mumbai

Copyright © Dan True 1994

First published in the USA by Blue Dolphin Publishing Inc. 1994.
This edition published by arrangement with the original publisher.

All rights reserved.
No part of this publication may be reproduced, transmitted, or stored in a retrieval system, in any form or by any means, electronic, mechanical, photocopying, recording or otherwise, without the prior permission of the publisher.

ISBN: 978-81-291-2467-8

10 9 8 7 6 5 4 3 2 1

The moral right of the author has been asserted.

This edition is for sale in the Indian Subcontinent only.

This book is sold subject to the condition that it shall not, by way of trade or otherwise, be lent, resold, hired out, or otherwise circulated, without the publisher's prior consent, in any form of binding or cover other than that in which it is published.

"Do not fancy every woman you meet as the heroine of a romance… avoid this error as you would shrink back from a precipice. And be not in haste to marry, or to engage your affections where there is no probability of a return. Of themselves, your fine sentiments and romantic notions will make no more impression on one of these delicate creatures than on a piece of marble. It is not what you think of them that determines their choice, but what they think of you."

—William Hazlitt

Contents

WHY THIS BOOK WAS WRITTEN		xiii
1	**MONEY, WOMEN, AND MEN**	1
	How do you respond to men who say that money is the number one thing you want from them?	2
	Would you rather your man have a job he is unhappy with that pays more than a job he likes that pays less?	3
	Which is more important to you, a man's present earning capacity, or his future earning potential?	4
	On a scale of zero to ten, how important is a man's social status in your dating or relationship choices?	6
	How do you think men feel about their woman having a job with higher pay and/or more prestige than theirs?	7
	How would you spend, or use, any larger amounts of surplus money you and your mate have left over?	8
	What does "being taken care of" mean to you? What do you think it means to the average man?	14

2 WOMEN TALK ABOUT RELATIONSHIPS
   WITH MEN   19
   What are the number one and number two items you
      want from marriage or a relationship with a man?   19
   If you discovered that your man had lied to you,
      what would be your reaction?   22
   When men and women don't get along smoothly,
      in your opinion, what are the primary causes
      of conflict?   25
   What can a man do that makes you feel good
      about yourself?   34
   What is your idea of an enjoyable way to spend time,
      such as an afternoon or evening, with a man?   37
   What can a man do that annoys you or makes you
      uncomfortable?   41
   Do you envy any qualities or traits you think are
      common to males in general?   45
   What is your opinion as to a weakness you consider
      common to males in general?   47
   Is your closest friend male or female, and why?   50
   Do you think some men fear women? If so, what
      do you think they fear?   51
   How do you think many men perceive women?   54
   On a scale of zero to ten, how important is it that
      you have an ongoing close friendship with a man?   57
   What is your definition of intimacy? What do you
      believe intimacy means to a man?   59
   When a man says he loves you, what does that mean
      to you?   61
   What attracts you to a man?   68
   Describe your version of a sexy man.   71
   What is your definition of a loving man?   75

3	**WOMEN TALK ABOUT MEN AND SEX**	**78**
	On a scale of zero to ten, how important is sex to you personally? How important is sex to a man, and is there a difference for you between having sex and making love?	79
	How do you feel about a husband believing he is entitled to sex with you on demand?	82
	How important is the size of a man's penis? Do you prefer large, or not so large?	84
	What do you get from sex?	86
	What do you want from sex?	91
	Do you have preferences as to who should initiate sex?	94
	On a scale of zero to ten, how important is orgasm?	96
	When you fail to have orgasm, what percentage of the problem do you assign to your partner?	100
	How do you feel about giving oral sex to a man, and how do you feel about receiving oral sex from a man?	102
	If you had to give up hugging and caressing FOREVER, or sex FOREVER, which would you give up? The key word is *forever*.	104
	What are your comments about other bed partners in your man's life: a) before you, and b) during his relationship with you?	107
	What could your husband do, or not do, that might cause you to consider a one night stand, or even an affair?	108
	How do you respond to a man, one who is unknown to you, ogling your body?	109
	How do you respond to a male you are intimate with ogling your body?	110

What are your feelings about a man who has *Playboy/Penthouse*/etc. AT THE TOP of his reading list?	111
Were you molested as a child, or raped at anytime in your life?	114
What is your level of concern about herpes (0-10), AIDS (0-10), and other STDs (0-10)?	116
At the time of your first sexual experience, for which reason did you choose to let it happen? a) romantic fulfillment, b) heat of passion, c) to deliberately lose virginity, d) curiosity, e) rape.	116
A few general comments offered by the one hundred women about sex.	**117**

4 WOMEN'S PSYCHE ABOUT MEN — **129**

What advice would you give a man who wants to get acquainted with you?	129
What are turn-offs when you first meet a man and are making up your mind about him?	132
*Does any special physical trait turn you on when you meet a man or see a man in the store, parking lot, office, or on a movie/TV screen? In other words, do you have a fixed idea of how the "ideal" man should look?	133
What could a man expect from you that you would dislike more than anything else?	135
What could a man do, unexpectedly, that would please or pleasantly surprise you?	138
How important is it that you and your mate have similar interests, or even like vocations?	139
What kind of relationship do you prefer your man have with his a) mother; b) sisters; c) daughters; d) ex-wife?	141

* One of three key questions. See pages 175 and 183 also.

In what order do you think men want the following
   from women?
   a) housekeeper/cook
   b) sex
   c) companionship 143
What order do you prefer? 143
On a scale of zero to ten, how important is it that
   your man have handyman skills? 144
How important is a sense of humor, on a scale of
   zero to ten? 145
How do you want a man to handle his anger? 146
If a man is open with you about his worries, is he
   weak or strong in your eyes? 147
What makes a man strong in your eyes? 149
Would you cut a smoker from your prospect list? 150
What are your comments about liquor and men? 151
What are your feelings about a man and foul language? .. 153
What are your comments about religion and the
   man you choose? 154
What are your comments on a man's refusal to insure
   himself to cover your financial needs in case of
   his death? 155
What is, or was, at the top of your list of likes about
   being single? 156
What did you dislike about being single? 157
How do you react to men who act macho? 158
What is your impression of men who brag a lot? 160
What makes a home a home? 161
How important is it that a part of your home be your
   space exclusively, on a scale of zero to ten? 163
How important is it that you occasionally have time
   to yourself? 163

What are your feelings about being dominated?	164
What are your comments about someone who makes you feel as if they own you?	166
Would you marry a man with faults you expect to change later?	168
If you could wave a magic wand and make one change in your man, what would you change?	170
What could your man do that would cause your disrespect and/or disappointment?	172
What is guaranteed to trigger resentment or a fight between you and your man?	173
*How late is tardy for an appointment or date with you? What is your most probable reaction when your date finally arrives, late?	175
Which is more important to you, a man's formal education or his intelligence?	178
What is the age of the man you want relative to your age?	180
Do you want a man taller or shorter than you? How much taller or shorter?	181
What do you think about a mustache? Like, dislike, makes no difference. Beard? Like, dislike, makes no difference.	182
*Since girlhood, have you had a life fantasy? If so, to what degree has that fantasy driven your adult life?	183
Looking back on all of your life's worth of experiences with men up to now, has the total of their influence on your life been a plus or a minus? Give examples of each.	186

5 MISCELLANEOUS NUGGETS OF WISDOM GLEANED FROM ONE HUNDRED WOMEN'S MINDS — 190

THE INTERVIEW QUESTIONS — 193

ACKNOWLEDGEMENTS — 201

* One of three key questions. See pages 133, 175, and 183.

Why This Book Was Written

In the months following my divorce, I kept asking myself, "What went wrong?" Both my former wife and I were above average in intelligence, and the mix of our personalities produced some pleasant years. Yet, a break came. Since it takes two to tango, we both shared whatever blame there was in the breakup. Nevertheless, I came to feel that if I had really known what she wanted, maybe we could have made it work.

When I realized we were in trouble, I read the latest books and articles on marriage and relationships. None, however, seemed to answer my question. At one point I considered doing my own research on what women want from men and writing my own book. But the fact that I have no doctorate or masters in that field subdued me. So I shelved the idea and got on with life. But the question persisted.

After a couple of years I decided simply to do the research for my personal use. I worked in television and was aware that statisticians for national TV rating services had established that a sample of a few hundred families from across the nation represented the viewing habits of our two hundred forty-eight million men, women, and children. Since my inquiry was aimed at only one family member, I felt reasonable accuracy could be achieved from interviewing one hundred women. So I bought a tape recorder, created a list of questions I thought were relevant, and marched ahead.

My original list contained thirty-seven questions. However, at the end of each interview I asked the woman to suggest questions she thought I should ask in future interviews. The women's additions expanded my list to one-hundred-and-ten questions. Eighty-two were selected for inclusion in this work. Some questions were extremely personal, yet were answered easily, with an openness that surprised me.

In the beginning, I interviewed friends and acquaintances, my former wife among them. After I exhausted those sources, I asked the women I had interviewed for referrals. In selecting interviewees, I chose women who represented all geographical areas of the United States, along with racial representations closely matching the ethnic mix of our population. The average age of the women was thirty-seven; the most mature individual was sixty-six. Their average level of education was 2.1 years of college.

As I compiled the work it occurred to me that the women I interviewed were the real authors. Their ideas and thoughts, often pithy and earthy, revealed a collective wisdom that may at least equal the wisdom of trained professionals. From their one hundred answers to each question I selected those which, in my opinion, produced the most useful information. To preserve the women's wisdom undiluted, and at the same time retain the flavor and spice of their minds, the work is presented using the women's words, with an occasional personal observation written by me. As a bonus from doing this book, three questions emerged that seemed to be quick, simple guides to increasing a man's chance for a successful relationship with an individual woman. In fact, if I were single, I would get answers to these three questions before I went beyond a second date. (See pages 133, 175, 183.) Information I gained from interviews with the one hundred women led me to understand why my former wife and I came to divorce. Had I (we) been smarter sooner, it is probable we would have never married. Now, since one hundred women have increased my understanding of the female mind, I have more confidence in my ability to select a partner more intelligently. Interviewing one hundred women was an *ah-ha* experience. I hope you enjoy peeking into their minds as much as I did.

In the process of writing this work, I discovered from one woman that early man didn't expect marriage to provide romance and intimacy, as we do now. Back then (in patriarchal societies), marriage was a device to consolidate territories, keep the peace, produce children for field work, and provide the convenience of a readily available sex partner (Hendrix, 1988). In other words, marriage "back then" was based more on necessity than because two people just couldn't live without each other.

Apparently, the *idea* of courtly, romantic love was born in the 14th century. Romance in that era consisted of the knight winning his lady love's favor. Then the two wrote letters and pined over each other, but they didn't marry. Instead, the knight rode off to battles. It was an unrequited, frustrating love, a forever-to-be-delayed love that could only be consummated in an afterlife. I was surprised to learn that it has been only within the last forty to sixty years that marriage has been based on romantic love in the U.S. There is a reason for that.

The luxury of marriage based on romantic love becomes fashionable *only* when society overcomes its basic survival needs. In many third world countries, where survival is still a struggle, arranged marriages continue to be the rule. An example is Pakistan's female ex-prime minister, Benazir Bhutto, who took her murdered father's place. Bhutto was a bright woman of the world, yet she had a marriage that was arranged when she was four. For such countries, romantic marriage remains the same as it was for knights and their loves—only a moonstruck gleam in the eye of most young people.

In modern societies that have solved most of the issues regarding survival, more and more citizens want and expect their emotional needs met, which is a relatively new factor in the marriage equation. Therein lie possible problems and/or opportunities. If couples desire solutions, relationship problems can be solved. If we learn what draws us into a relationship, it becomes easier to learn skills that will help make that union run more smoothly over a longer period of time. The bonus is that such a relationship can be very rewarding and life-enriching for both partners. As with many new ideas, a lot has yet to be learned about marriage based on romantic attraction. At best, such a marriage is still experimental. (Can you point to one marriage that you consider "perfect"?) Besides, with so many marriages in "first world" countries failing, obviously we don't have all of the answers.

Although the women's answers in this survey speak about men, their thoughts and words revealed their inner selves … their values, emotions, and motivations. To tap into those feelings, when the moment seemed right I encouraged individual women to "tell John Doe exactly how you feel in your heart of hearts." At those times, many of the women's private, innermost thoughts were shared and recorded. Males and females alike can gain knowledge, draw strengths, and derive the benefit of experience from these women's candid, eloquent opinions.

This book is respectfully presented with the hope that men and women can become more confident and assertive about what they *do* want, and how they might better handle themselves in the process of cultivating and maintaining a relationship.

1

Money, Women, and Men

AT A HOTEL BAR in Albuquerque, New Mexico, I was talking with a single female co-worker about the differences that sometimes arise between men and women. Other men and women within earshot were eavesdropping. At one point I asked my co-worker, "What do women really want from men?"

Next to me a man slapped the bar and guffawed, "They want money, dummy."

After laughter had subsided he hoisted his glass. Before taking a swig he added, "Any idiot knows that."

Male chuckles followed, along with other hoisted glasses and "Hear-hears." Females frowned. I turned to my woman friend. "How do you respond to that?"

She surveyed the men. "Did any of you notice the silver BMW in the parking lot?" After only a second she added, "It's mine … bought and paid for by me." She looked from man to man. "You may think women are after your money. But what some of you may not have noticed is that many women don't need your money … we have the ability to make our own. We don't need yours for survival."

That simple exchange prompted me to push on with the writing of this book. In forging ahead, I asked the one hundred women several questions about money and men. The first was the one that was born in the bar:

How do you respond to men who say that money is the number one thing you want from them?

A THIRTY-ONE-YEAR-OLD MOTEL NIGHT CLERK answered, "Bullcorn. I will live with a man in a pup tent in a pasture and eat dandelions and rabbits. I'll work side by side with him, so long as he loves me, respects me, and treats me decently. That's what's important to me ... not his money."

A four-foot-eleven-inch, 103-pound thirty-six-year-old said she thought the money question was more important to a man than a woman. "Men seem to need possessions. Women might lay that money thing to rest if they decline to take the man's name and keep theirs, *and* their job."

A financial counselor's opinion was, "Some women do want a man's money, but I think those are women who are shallow in their own development—in other words, airheads. I won't put energy into dealing with a man who thinks I'm after his money. If he thought that, I'd wonder in what other dumb ways he views women. I'd be an idiot to let a man like that into my life."

An accountant had a different view of money and men. "I expect him to contribute his share of earnings. I have no problem with earning my share. In fact, I've always made more than my husband and wound up giving him money. But I expect my man to bring home a paycheck. And money ranks with my wish for him to be an honest person. I want both money and honesty. But if he doesn't bring home a paycheck, forget it. I don't want an honest bum."

A forty-five-year-old psychotherapist said, "At my age, my idea is different than when I was twenty-five. Then, a man's money meant that he could take care of me. Today I know that money doesn't really represent taking care of me. To 'take care of me' means to give me emotional support (see page 9). I have a bigger view of life than money. Money isn't something I see as a man's responsibility."

A forty-nine-year-old defense plant services manager said, of men thinking that women want money, "Bullshit. My first husband was successful at making money. He was considered the breadwinner, but my salary raised our standard of living. Without giving me any credit, he silently acted as though he depended on my check. So tell me, who was after whose money?"

An advertising agency owner said, "I brought money into my second marriage. He was a wheeler-dealer with my money. After he spent me broke, and I divorced and recovered financially, it verified what I suspected ... I can take care of my financial needs. I don't need a man for money, or one to manage *mine*."

A forty-three-year-old marriage counselor said, "A lot of men come to me with financial insecurities. That's devastating for men, because they equate wealth with power, self esteem, privilege, and success. That men think women want money from them doesn't surprise me. But men should ask women what they want from marriage or a relationship (see page 19), instead of presuming what they want or expect from him."

"His money might be nice, but it's in last place, behind devotion, emotional support, and companionship." She paused and added, "Look at the rich people who are miserable in their marriages—proof that money alone doesn't create happiness."

In an attempt to increase the accuracy of the women's answers, I sprinkled the money questions throughout the interview. My intent was to put enough space between each question to provide the women with a fresh turn of thought and, hopefully, fresh answers. My next money question was:

Would you rather your man have a job he is unhappy with that pays more than a job he likes that pays less?

NINETY-NINE PERCENT of the women said they wanted their man happy with his job, even if it meant earning less. Some of their comments were:

A bank executive secretary said, "At his last job, which paid well, he was unhappy and dissatisfied. I didn't object when he said he wanted to leave it. In his new job, which pays less, he's a lot easier to live with."

A forty-one-year-old courier for an air freight company said, "My husband was a manager, but didn't like the hassle, so he stepped down a notch and took a pay cut. I was thrilled, because I got my husband back. The trade-off for money wasn't worth the unhappiness."

A Santa Fe shop owner pointed out, "If part of your job really eats you, and it colors your life, it's not worth the bother. I wouldn't want anything less for him than for me. I want him to have a job he likes that may pay less, rather than see him with higher pay while miserable and full of stress."

A blonde, twenty-nine-year-old housewife believes, "If he's happy with his work, he's happy with everything else in his life. If his life is better, so is mine. Then he won't come home and take out his job frustrations out on me, the kids, or the cat."

The one woman out of the hundred who voted for her husband to keep a job he didn't like said, "If he's making tons of money but is not happy, for him to use his unhappiness as a reason to become a ditch digger will not make me real happy."

Although men seem to have a mandate from the women to like their jobs, several of the women said they didn't want a workaholic either. One of them put it this way: "I want him to care about his work, but I don't want a workaholic." She added, "Men give women so little time anyway … unless they are out to get them into bed—don't give me a workaholic to boot."

A forty-five-year-old teacher summed up how most of the women felt about their husband's jobs: "Hey, he comes home from work to me. I want him to walk in smiling."

Clearly, if the woman has a choice between a man being happy or rich, she'll probably opt for seeing him happy. So far, they seem consistent on their stated view of men and money—and they seem willing to deliver on campaign promises.

My third money question was:

Which is more important to you, a man's present earning capacity, or his future earning potential?

SIXTY-FOUR PERCENT of the women rated future earning potential as more important, while twenty-two percent preferred a man's present earning capacity. Fourteen percent said it made no difference. Younger women tended to answer differently than older women. For example, a forty-four-year-old said: "A man's age will make a difference in that question. When I was younger, his future potential was more important. But as I get older, present becomes more important to me."

The wife of a construction firm owner said she preferred "future earning potential, because if he is the best ice cream soda maker in town, at some point in his future he will make top dollar as an ice cream soda maker. I want a guy who wants to be the best at whatever he does. I want a guy who doesn't whine about problems, but jumps in and fixes them instead. That attitude says he's mentally strong. With a guy like that, the money part will almost automatically take care of itself."

A doctor's wife said, "I don't care what he makes. I wouldn't care if he was a ditch digger, attorney, or president. As long as he has good values coupled with drive, his income at the moment is unimportant, because this guy's future is going to be good."

The motel clerk liked a man's potential earning capacity, because "what's inside of him is important to me. If he has no goals, no character, etc., I won't get involved because I don't want a bum. At the same time, I won't push him. He must be self-motivated. What he chooses to do is a matter for his heart, not mine. When I meet him, how we respond and interact is more important than him having big earnings. If he has heart and we are on the same frequency, his, really *our*, future earning potential will be high."

One woman answered, "If he is making money and has money in the bank, that's a sure sign he's a man. I like that idea."

A television camera-person said that neither present pay nor future earning potential was high on her list. "Intelligence is what I want. If he's got a good mind, earning capacity will come. Meanwhile, while he's getting there, I've got the advantage of being with someone who has a sharp mind."

A thirty-seven-year-old author/speaker said, "I don't care what he's capable of earning, even if he has to collect bottles and cans, so long as he's *trying*."

The television reporter said, "I was in a relationship because I thought the guy had potential, and that down the line it was all going to be okay. Well, he was not highly motivated, and having him in my life sucked. Today, I want concrete results, not dream potential. I don't want a guy whose tombstone is going to read, 'But he had great potential.'"

Another woman said, "If you make a million a year but go home and pour your happiness from a bottle into a glass, as far as I'm concerned, you're not successful. I would trade an unhappy millionaire for a happy minimum-wage guy. I want us to smell the flowers and enjoy the sunsets."

Since money and social status are often interconnected, I asked the women:

On a scale of zero to ten, how important is a man's social status in your dating or relationship choices?

On a scale of zero to ten, 4.3 was the average that one hundred women placed on a man's social status. The values assigned ranged from "minus five" to "plus fifteen."

A forty-one-year-old client service rep for a temporary help firm said, "Social status doesn't carry much weight with me. I simply want a man who communicates with others and gets along with any level of society, from janitors to bank presidents. I don't want to have to guide him through a social event. But his social status isn't important."

A thirty-seven-year-old lawyer said, "Idealistically, I'd say I could date a ditch digger. Problem is, I couldn't respect him, because I think a man who is a ditch digger is that mostly by choice. I think he could be more if he wanted to expend the effort. His lack of motivation prejudices me. On your scale, I'm a seven."

"A few years ago it would have been zero," said an accountant. "Now it's a seven or eight. I've learned that if a man has no social status, it is a statement about his personality. It may signal that he is introverted, or withdrawn, or whatever. If he's like that outside the home, he's probably going to be that way within the home. On the other hand, if a man has social status, that tells me he is probably enjoyable to be with anywhere."

A housewife said, "People who are interesting tend to do interesting things. Some of them run backhoes, fight forest fires, or fly jet fighters. A man's social status isn't important, so long as he is interesting and growing."

One of the marriage counselors observed: "I wish I could say that social status has no relevance. But, when I was young and crazily enamored with a man, I foolishly asked him what he did. When he said he drove a trash truck, I suddenly discovered I was more of a snob than I thought. Until that moment, I considered myself as pretty egalitarian. Since flunking that test, social status settled on a rating of six or seven, and that is based more on how he is regarded in his community than the amount of money he commands."

A motel night clerk said, "It's not how *high* he is on the social ladder, but rather how *low* he is. Unknown to me, my second husband had a four-and-a-half page rap sheet. I'm not looking for a man who is wealthy or a social butterfly, because men like that too often tend to be too wrapped up in where they are and what they must do to hold their position. They don't have time to be loving. They're too occupied with themselves to be any fun."

A forty-four-year-old antique shop owner said, "If you mean, do I want a man who is competent, secure in himself, and has imagination coupled with drive, the answer is yes. Show me any man with that, and I'll show you a man with status. You bet. I'll take him, status and all, in a New York minute."

These money questions were asked when our national economy was "up." Women who read this section during the "recession" said they believed that a woman who had fallen on hard financial times might marry Godzilla if Godzilla had money. Even so, it appears that, over all, their answers continue to reflect how they claim they feel about men and money.

The fifth question I asked about men and money was:

How do you think men feel about their woman having a job with higher pay and/or more prestige than theirs?

A FORTY-FIVE-YEAR-OLD CALIFORNIA TEACHER answered, "I think that's scary for most men. Most men feel they should be taller, smarter, and make more money than a woman. It takes a very secure man to be comfortable with a woman who has more of any of the above."

A forty-one-year-old personnel manager said, "Even if they repeat over and over that it doesn't bother them, I don't believe them. I think deep down they are bothered and feel looked down on in the woman's eyes and in the eyes of their friends. To make it worse, sometimes their male friends make snide little remarks, like 'is she traveling again?' Or they'll rub it in by asking about other neat things she does that he doesn't do in his job."

A forty-seven-year-old believed, "They may talk the talk, but they can't walk the walk. Underneath, I think they resent their woman making more than them. It may go back to Biblical times when the man is described as head of the house. If his wife earns more than he does, he might wonder what he is and why he is there. I think he worries that she doesn't need him anymore."

A bank executive secretary said, "I think it scares them. They fear that if a woman makes more than they do, that shadows their masculinity. That's stupid ... his masculinity should depend on his self-image. If he were a mechanic at Joe's garage, secure in himself, his wife or girlfriend making more than him wouldn't bother him." She smiled. "But those men are rare."

A twenty-eight-year-old manager said, "How he reacts to that situation depends on his intelligence. If he can deal with it, he's a man for me. Otherwise, I'm not going to lower my standards."

A twenty-seven-year-old bank teller said, "The secure type will applaud her. The insecure type will climb the walls."

A forty-year-old night manager of a convenience store thought, "A man who can handle his wife making more than him is manly and masculine, and he turns me on."

Notice that these women held a tolerant view about a man making less than his wife. And they continued to be consistent in their stated positions about money and men. Nevertheless, peace and tranquility may be strained in homes where she makes more than he does. For example, studies show that the divorce rate for couples where she earned more than he did was fifty percent higher than for couples in which the man earned more than his wife (Cherlin, 1981; Whyte, 1990; Fisher, 1992). It would be interesting to see a study identifying which mate is more likely to initiate divorce proceedings in households where she makes the most.

My next question in the money series was:

How would you spend, or use, any larger amounts of surplus money that you and your mate have left over?

SIXTY-SEVEN PERCENT of the women answered, "Travel." The secretary said, "I'd use the money to travel—around the world if there was enough. I feel that travel is an investment in yourself. Travel is a positive experience. I come back from a trip smarter. Also, a trip makes beautiful memories. For example, compare using the money to buy things, such as a silver service. Rather than travel I could sit home with my shiny silver, and not become one iota smarter—and polishing silver isn't likely to give me wonderful memories. On the other hand, traveling fills our heads with warm memories to share in front of an evening fire for the rest of our lives."

An Associated Press photographer said, "It's important that I have quality time with my partner. A lot of couples fall into the trap of wanting to provide. In the process they have very little time together, and when they do have time, both are so tired from the rigors of the rat race, they can't have much fun. I would use surplus money to get away from it all—travel to some out of the way place, away from the tourist herd."

A housewife and family business bookkeeper said, "When I was younger, I would have used surplus money to redecorate my house. Now, travel is my first choice."

Of the twenty-eight percent of the women who voted for investing their surplus money, one said, "Why does it have to be spent? Save it. My philosophy is, buy nothing you want and only half of what you need."

Three percent of the women would give a portion of any surplus money to charity. One said, "I would find some little old couple or little old lady who is barely making it on social security. After I saw that their basic needs were met, then I would provide things beyond creature comforts."

A twenty-nine-year-old vice president of a flying service said she would buy a Cessna Citation jet. I tallied her preference about using surplus money under "travel."

For a professional opinion about money, men, and women, I talked with a forty-eight-year-old marriage counselor. She said, "Money in the relationship symbolizes concentrated energy, energy most likely born from the relationship. Money arguments usually are about how that concentration of energy is going to be used: Who is going to have access? What is 'our' energy going to be used for? Do we both want what a particular use of the energy might produce?" The counselor advised, "Instead of arguing about money, try discussing how the two of you can maximize the use of 'our' energy for the mutual pleasure or well-being of both."

It appears that these women have given the money issue more thought than many men believe. Clearly, women's earning capacities give them options, including the choice to live independently and single. That makes many of my men friends uneasy, uneasy because it also allows the woman in their life to depart if she so desires. In the history of civilization, women have had that option for a relatively short time, primarily during the last fifty years or so. Before that, males and females often paired off because of what I call "built-in dependency," an idea that came to me from observing the lives of a pair of golden eagles.

Female eagles are twenty percent larger than male eagles. Since male eagles are smaller, they are the family's fighter plane, and are expected to defend the territory. Because of his smaller size, he is also designated as the pair's nest builder. The theory behind his assignment is, since the birds take turns at egg-brooding duty, if the female built the nest, his small size might allow snowy, chilly winds to threaten eggs in a nest cup he can't tightly cover during his turn (see page 93 of *A Family of Eagles* by Dan True, University of New Mexico Press). The difference in size between male and female eagles also impacts other aspects of their relationship. Believing there is a reason for everything in nature, I wondered, "Why has nature designed men to be larger and stronger than women? Even more important," I wondered, "how does our size and strength differential affect our relationships?" Since humans seem driven more by biology than sociology, to go back to man's earliest days seemed a logical beginning. I envisioned a caveman environment.

My mind's eye pictured a lone, animal-skin-clad male sitting inside a cave, roasting a leg of venison. Snow covered the frozen-solid ground. Within half an hour the sun would set.

My mind's eye shifted to a point a half a mile away. A nearly starved female was moving silently from cedar bush to cedar bush, stalking a deer. Her ribs showed, and her face was thin. When she was as near as she could get, she desperately launched an arrow from her bow at the animal. The arrow hit its mark, but barely penetrated the deer's skin. The deer bounded away. Her caved-in stomach rumbled. Unconsciously she fingered her empty herb and root pouch, cursed the frozen ground, shivered, and paused to regroup. Through sunken eyes she scanned the frozen land. Her stomach rumbled again. She brushed hair from her face and in the distance spotted smoke rising from the caveman's fire. Stumbling forward, she plodded through the snow toward the smoke.

Near dark, the female peered from behind a bush a few yards from the caveman. Muscular, robust, and well-fed, he sat against a boulder beside his fire. His feet were crossed and he picked venison from his teeth with a wooden splinter. The cave's floor was littered with flint chips and wood shavings. A tattered article of clothing made from animal skins, which he had been repairing, rested on his lap. His bow, larger and more powerful than hers, lay within easy reach, next to several arrows. She began to feel that if she hadn't been built with so much less muscle-power than a man, she could pull a more powerful bow and her arrow might have penetrated the deer enough to bring it down. She envied the strength that seemed to be a male birthright. A leftover roast rested on a rock some distance away from the fire. The woman swallowed. Her throat was dry. Quietly she sneaked in as close as she dared, then rushed forward, grabbed the roast, ran a few yards out into the gathering darkness and ravenously ate her fill.

Two hours later the caveman and cavewoman were sitting before the fire. Under the spell of their shared evening, they decided it might be mutually advantageous to remain together. Their agreement was, she would keep the fire going, tan and sew raw hides into clothing, and keep the cave tidy. He would make bows and arrows and hunt. "An instant family" I mused, and wondered if our man-woman size differential was purposely designed to force ancestral men and women to pair-bond through depending upon each other. However, caveman life, at least in colder climes, seemed stacked against females, making them more dependent on a male partner for survival than vice versa. So I rewound my mental tape back to where the female was stalking the deer.

On my replay, I envisioned a fantasy caveman era, wherein all females were exactly equal in size and strength to males. To repeat, the woman in my new scene was strong, healthy, and physically as powerful as any man. This man-sized woman launched a fast-flying arrow that successfully got the deer. The caveman heard the ruckus and stormed out to see what was going on in "his" territory. When he found the female skinning the deer, he roared, "What are you doing with my deer?"

A knock-down-drag-out fight over the animal followed. During the battle she killed the caveman and returned to skinning her deer, which she was soon cooking in his cave. After her meal, she picked venison from her teeth with a splinter taken from his fire wood. Obviously, no family will come out of the meeting between this man and woman. My hypothesis: an ancestral woman as physically powerful as ancestral man might have threatened the long-term survival of our species.

Modern technology has made women, economically, *almost* as big and *almost* as strong as men. Educated, healthy, and robust, today's women take powerful shots at good-paying jobs on the hunting grounds of corporate America. The fact that a woman often "bags" a job has made her less dependent upon a male.

Now that women aren't forced to pair with a man for survival, they can opt to remain single. Since birth control methods release them from the fear and burden of impregnation, these women are free to have sex with anyone, anytime, if they so choose. Probably for the first time in human history, women can get by with treating men simply as sex objects, in the same way that, for millions of years, many men looked upon women as "things."

For a lot of men, finding the shoe on the other foot is confusing, frustrating, and disturbing. Adding to men's stress is the fact that a woman they may worship, and want to have children by, can shop in a sperm bank for genes she considers superior to his. At her whim, she can inseminate herself without ever going to bed with him, and proceed to raise a family alone.

One bright, attractive comptroller who earns more than many men put her view of a modern woman's life into perspective when she observed: "With Jim, I have a four-year exclusive relationship, plus a four-year non-exclusive. We live separately, but I'll be fine if we marry, or I'll be fine if we don't."

Jim, nervous about the other men in her life, wanted marriage. She insisted on the freedom to pursue her lifestyle. At the end of their eighth year, Jim called to say good-bye, that he was engaged to marry a person he recently met.

The comptroller easily found a new man, landed an even better job, and took a second man to keep in the wings as insurance against her new man repeating Jim's action. Happily single and intending to remain so, she continues to live mostly alone in a large, fine home. Being able to provide for herself clearly gives this woman options that were not available to most females only a couple of generations ago.

Another effect that women's increasing independence may have on relationships is reflected in the comments of a beautiful, financially-independent, single woman whom I met after this survey was completed. She said that the minute a man discovers she is financially secure, and doesn't work, he seems threatened. Invariably he changes from suitor to combatant, and attacks her self-esteem and/or puts her down in subtle ways. Wistfully, she added, "While my biological clock is ticking louder and louder, romance is dead before it has a chance to blossom."

Is it possible that modern technology may be going against nature's plan of designing men and women unequal in strength and size? Is it possible that the increase in violence by men toward women is driven by men who feel threatened or who have been displaced from jobs by a woman? It may seem farfetched, but is it possible that a percentage of the apparent increase in rapes result from jobless men who have been reduced in status with a subsequent reduction in consensual sexual access to females? Is on-the-job harassment by males of female co-workers, including "making life miserable for her," in part a result of competition from women? Are current divorce rates connected to the changing status of women in modern society? I'll leave answers to those questions to you, the sociologists, and the anthropologists.

Please understand I'm making observations, not judgments. I think it's wonderful that women have opportunities to be all that they can. Also, after having been to war, I believe the world might be better served if every country on the planet were headed by a woman. At the same time, it appears there may be social costs attached to the advancement of women. Answers may lie in the question, "How can we minimize possible social costs while maximizing women's opportunities?"

Although I have proposed a theory and made observations on some possible *effects* on the relationships between men and women because of man/woman size/muscle differential, I haven't addressed the question of *how* we came by this size difference. In the beginning, were Adam and Eve equal, or was Adam deliberately designed stronger than Eve, and both genetically imprinted to propagate that pattern perpetually? In other words, have our male and female genes been instructed to grow human males larger and stronger than females? Or could selective forces be behind our size differences? This idea led me to some humorous thoughts on the subject. With tongue in cheek, please consider the two paragraphs which follow.

After interviewing one hundred women, I have concluded that, overall, they have more "world smarts" than males. Humorously, because my male ego demands that it be humorous, I wonder if selective forces at work within men caused us to choose females who are smaller and physically less powerful than we as mates. I mean, if females do have more "world smarts," add that to their being just as big and powerful as men, and there goes the patriarchal hierarchy—there goes the neighborhood. Under those conditions, males the world over might be *totally* dominated by women. In other words, if females are at once the smartest *and* the biggest, it would probably be a woman's world. So, again I wondered: is it possible that selective forces driven by male survival (or ego) strategies have encouraged men to choose smaller, less powerful women to mate with, which has resulted in breeding the size of the smart women down? There may be another side to that coin.

Maybe the majority of women's sexual strategies, from the beginning of human history, have been to mate with larger, muscular men in order to acquire greater "protection" and the benefits of hunting (paycheck) prowess. Across the generations, such a strategy should have resulted in a population of males who are bigger and stronger than females. Coincidentally, such mating choices might unwittingly have trapped cave-era females into the dilemma of forced dependency. Whether these off-the-wall ideas have merit or not, the question remains: Why are men bigger and stronger than women, and has that affected male/female relationships? (The answer I hear most is, "Men are bigger and stronger because they must both hunt and defend their families against enemies." However, if the female were as big as an elephant, so long as she is a spectator, her size would have no bearing on the outcome of her mate's hunting powers or his battles against invaders.)

This question leads directly to the issue of "being taken care of." From interviewing these women, I learned that men and women often have differing definitions of important subjects. Sensing that "being taken care of" might be one of those subjects, I asked the women:

What does "being taken care of" mean to you? What do you think it means to the average man?

NINETY-FIVE PERCENT of the women said they believed a man's definition of taking care of a woman was based on providing money for material needs. Sixty-one percent said *their* primary definition of being taken care of was having their *emotional* needs met. Financial security rated second with thirty-nine percent of the women.

Here's how a thirty-one-year-old lawyer put it: "Most men think they are taking care of you by providing for you financially. However, for a woman, being taken care of means having her emotional needs met first, with financial needs in second place. I'm not being taken care of when someone simply throws money at me. He also must listen to my problems and be someone I can readily talk to. I don't want simply to be taken care of materially. I can do that very well myself. To be taken care of properly, I must be well fed emotionally."

A forty-one-year-old escrow officer said, "To be taken care of means I have a man who is sensitive to my needs or hurts ... my emotions. Give me emotional support and care, and you've taken care of me."

The motel clerk said, "When my world gets shaky, or when my day has been long, or when my eyes look like a caged cat and my back and feet hurt, and he comes to me and says, 'Let me hold you.' That's my idea of being taken care of."

The widow of a night freighter pilot has shifted her definition of being taken care of. She said, "Since I lost him, I realize sharply his importance as the emotional pillar in my life."

I asked this woman, "Before his death, did you weigh financial security above emotional support?"

Her answer was, "Yes. I wasn't aware of the importance of emotional security until after he was gone. Now, I treasure and value the emotional security I got from the marriage, more than the financial security."

When I interviewed a doctor's wife, her husband was present. Before posing the question to her, I asked his opinion of what taking care of his wife encompassed. He answered, "I provide her with the necessities of life."

His wife looked at him. "Honey bunch, I hate to rain on your parade, but I can provide *material* necessities myself... I don't need you for that."

The doctor looked surprised. She went on, "*Taking care of me* means that when I'm emotionally hurt, you have the guts to put your arms around me and reassure me." She snuggled close to him. "*That's* taking care of me."

He and I exchanged quick glances, and I moved on to the next question.

A forty-one-year-old diagnostic technician said, "Taking care of me is giving me moral and mental support. Without that, I don't have a relationship." She added, "Also, I like to help put a roof over our heads and food on the table."

A different outlook came from the secretary for a utility company. She explained, "Taking care of me includes my everyday well-being, my emotional well-being, and my financial needs for survival. That may sound mercenary, but it's not. There is a great deal to be said for a man wanting to work enough to provide creature comforts that make a home a home. It's something a man can do that many women cannot, unless they inherited financial security, or are clever or talented and can convert cleverness or talent into dollars." She was silent a moment, before adding: "And remember, sir, that a lot of women and children live in poverty simply because women don't make equal pay ... equal to a man's."

A thirty-seven-year-old psychologist and author said, "Self-sufficiency is my solution to somebody taking care of me. I'll take care of myself, and I want a man who can take care of himself. If he can't do that, he sure can't take care of me. I haven't seen many men who can take care of themselves, or women either for that matter. Everybody is looking for a mom."

A detective story writer said, "Once a woman is a complete person within herself, then she can have a relationship with a man. But it is not fair for a woman to place the responsibility for her happiness on the men or man in her life. I feel that, number one, I need to look out for myself. If I'm happy in what I'm doing and treating myself physically and mentally well, then, to have a man in my life is a delightful addition. He adds a masculine touch in caring, loving, and being supportive. But I shouldn't expect him to create my happiness. That's my job."

The thirty-nine-year-old financial counselor said, "My first reaction is, yes, it would be wonderful to be taken care of and have that security blanket. That could be interpreted to mean I was wanted and desired, which would reduce my anxieties. *On the other hand*, I don't think its healthy to depend on someone to take care of me, because I really need to take care of myself on a core level first. I feel I must learn to look out for myself on all levels. Then, the addition of a good relationship would be gravy ... a benefit ... a bonus added to what I already have. Rather than needing a man to make me a whole person, a man would add to what I already have going. His addition could make my life more pleasant and more enjoyable."

My comment was, "It's obvious you don't like the idea of being taken care of ... that you'd rather take care of yourself."

"That's right. I want to be self-sufficient. I want to take care of my practical needs myself. And I want to be emotionally strong from within myself. I want to make my own decisions, such as purchasing a car, insurance, etc., rather than depend on someone else. I want to make the everyday decisions, even though I may be wrong. I want to be able to make my own mistakes and have the joy of learning from them. This is a real issue for me, because I had a brother who made all my college decisions, 'so that I wouldn't make mistakes.' Well, I had a masters degree in three-and-a-half years by his steering me clear of roadblocks, so I graduated with a lot of class smarts, but no world smarts. I was twenty-one when I stepped into the real world. I felt as if I had been shot out of a cannon. Not only did I not have a course to follow, I didn't even know how to set a course, because he had done all my navigating. For years I floundered around, hitting reefs and crashing into rocky cliffs because I hadn't learned how to avoid hazards on my own. I wish that my brother had let me learn from my mistakes in college rather than navigating me around them. I needed those mistakes for their teaching value in order to make it in the real world. My brother denied me a chance for some important learning. So, I see dangers in being taken care of by someone else. To go a step further, if the caretaker becomes incapacitated or dies, or if there is a divorce, I see problems for the person who is being taken care of.

A twenty-nine-year-old photographer said, "In a relationship, a woman who isn't being taken care of emotionally is not being taken care of. A lot of men put their energy into providing material things. Then they feel nothing else is necessary. But for me, if a male isn't there emotionally, listening to my worries, sharing my dreams, or bringing me chicken soup when I'm ill, he isn't there."

A forty-three-year-old marriage counselor said, "I can't afford to pin my hopes on being taken care of by someone else. People die, move away, go through their own emotional battles, and become mentally absent from me for a period of time."

This observation was made by a forty-three-year-old teacher: "The words 'being taken care of' sound stifling. Being taken care of implies ownership. You take care of things you own ... car, dog, house, etc. I don't want to be owned. The difference is, and listen closely: you may either take care of a person, or you may care for that person. I prefer to be cared for. An experience on Love Field in Dallas highlights the difference.

"Two well-dressed guys and two well-dressed women had just deplaned from a small private jet and were standing with their luggage in the lobby. The two guys were discussing a business problem when one of the women moved in and said she had some insight into the problem. One of the fellows turned to her, and in a thick southern accent said, 'Honey, we'll take care of the deductive reasoning, Y'all take care of the seductive reasoning.' That is ownership ... I'm taking care of you (and therefore own you), so don't get into my business."

I admit that my definition of taking care of a woman has been knocked cockeyed by their answers. At the same time I note with interest that what they say matches their attitudes about men/women/money. But why do many of today's males, like those in the Albuquerque hotel bar, continue to believe that, "Women want money from men, dummy."

From humankind's beginnings 4.4 million years ago (*Nature* magazine, Sept. 1994), men have taken for granted that females had little choice but to depend upon a male for material support. However, the two world wars, and especially the second, opened good-paying defense jobs to women. Those jobs allowed women to crack an economic ceiling that previous generations of females had bumped their heads against. For the first time in human history, economic self-reliance became operative for large numbers of women.

The women I interviewed indicated that many men cling to outdated attitudes about women being able to support themselves. The women said that as a general rule, younger men seemed less inoculated by pre-twentieth-century male thinking about women and money. And from answers the women gave to money questions, it's obvious they understand the balance of relationship power generated by their economic status. The women also seemed impatient with men who found it hard to comprehend that women *really don't* need a man's money.

That said, I also met many working women who are tired of the rat race. Some said they would gladly swap their economic independence to manage a household, if only they could continue their family's standard of living on one (his) paycheck.

2

Women Talk about Relationships with Men
(Including Reasons Why They Believe We Sometimes Fight)

Since a *man's money* seems less important to modern women, then what do modern women want? I asked the question directly:

What are the number one and number two items you want from marriage or a relationship with a man?

"Honesty" topped the list of what women say they want from men. That was a surprise to me, so I began asking, "Why?" Invariably the reason was, "If he's honest, chances are everything else about a relationship will fall into place." Makes sense. Following honesty, the women want:

Love
Affection
Companionship
Romance
Good sex (See the chapter on SEX, page 78)
Intimacy (See page 59. A woman's definition is different from a man's.)
Communication

Only two respondents out of the one hundred rated money at the top of their lists. Other comments about what women wanted most were:

"I want to know there is not another human being he shares himself with more than me, and I don't mean sharing himself just on a physical level. I mean sharing the emotional aspects of his life with me ... the mental sharing. That is the number one thing I want from marriage ... the mental sharing. That's not to imply that I wouldn't wreak hell and havoc if he was giving himself physically to another woman. That would hurt my pride, but it wouldn't destroy my love. However, his sharing with her the innermost thoughts of his brain would destroy my love."

To this I responded, "I'm surprised that you would be less mad at his physical sharing than at his mental sharing."

"His mind is more private than his body. A body can be raped, but not a mind. A mind has to be given willingly. For him to share his innermost being with another female would devastate me."

When I asked what was the second most important item she would want from marriage, this woman replied, "A good lover. A man who understands how females are built... what my clitoris is (see page 118) and its importance in my complete sexual satisfaction. A good lover is sensitive to my needs and either knows how to satisfy me or is willing to follow my gentle requests."

This woman's thoughts on the traits of a good lover were echoed by several other women.

A twenty-nine-year-old secretary said, "I want nothing more than for him to be there. I want his friendship. I don't need his money ... I have a good job. By friendship, I mean I want him to talk to me, and I want him to hear me when I talk, and for us to respond to each other. I want closeness to his thoughts ... serious, total closeness to what's on his mind.

"The second most important item is good sex, which is sex that leaves me fulfilled and satisfied ... and that doesn't necessarily mean I have to have an orgasm every time." (See page 96).

A thirty-nine-year-old television personality said her number one want from a man is honesty: "The truth, for God's sake. I don't know how to relate to you if I don't know the truth. If the truth is going to hurt me, then it's going to hurt. But lying will be ten times more hurtful. If you tell the truth, I'll come up with a way to deal with the situation, but I can't deal intelligently with lies and deceit. I would rather have no information than false information, because I can make decisions on real information and come close to expected results. But decisions based on misinformation are off course from the start. For example, if you give me directions from Dallas to Houston that are 180° off course, I'll have to circle around the world to get there. That's an awful lot of unnecessary time and energy. Truth makes our trip through life so much easier, so much more predictable, and so much more pleasant.

"The second most important item I want from marriage is a toss-up between affection and intellect."

A blonde accountant also said honesty was the number one item she wanted. "Good, bad, or otherwise, tell me the truth. If you don't like me fat, tell me you don't like me fat. I may not do anything about it, but at least I know where you're coming from. If you don't like the color of carpet I selected, say so. Then I'll know why you turn up your nose when you walk through that room. I've wasted half my life and too much energy trying to figure out what a man is thinking. We could save a lot of energy and time if he'll just tell me. He can tell me in ten seconds what may take me ten days or ten years to figure out. Men are cowards when they don't truthfully say what they feel."

One woman I interviewed said she expected her man "to carry his own weight. I don't want a relationship where he is dependent, except within certain bounds. If he's overly dependent on me, I call that the long tit syndrome, and my tit will only stretch so far. I don't need somebody like that. Children do it, and it's okay because they are children. But I want no male with a long tit need."

A motel night clerk said she wanted, "A shoulder to cry on. A port in a storm. Warm arms to hold me when the world gets shaky … somebody to smile at me and pat me on the back when I've done well. Somebody who is not too busy to notice me when I'm good, bad, or indifferent."

To share with you how different individual women can be, listen to this twenty-six-year-old brunette: "I expect my husband to read my mind, without my having to talk to him. I want him to do things without me having to tell him. Men know what they can help you with, but it is easier for them to slip out the back door and pretend they don't know." This lady also wants "companionship, respect, love, understanding, and more sharing of emotional feelings than most men show."

Here's an answer that shows women change with time. "What I want from a man has changed. When I was younger, I wanted him only as a ticket to get away from home. At that point I was emotionally dependent, because life was freaking me out and I needed someone, *anyone*, to lean on. Now that I'm older and have grown up emotionally, I can take care of myself. Now I want a man I enjoy being with. That means he must be really intelligent. I want a man I can delight in and love to be with, someone who has ideas about things to do that are enjoyable, someone who puts himself out for me, or takes me places I enjoy. Obviously, my priority has changed as I've gotten older."

"Respect" is what a forty-two-year-old television station sales manager wants most of all, "respect for me as a person, not just as a piece of ass. Our relationship started as totally sexual, but out of that has come a really good mutual respect.

"The second most important item is loving attention. A lot of physical contact. That can be just hugging and touching ... watching TV with a head in a lap. Physical contact. That's real big with me."

One female I interviewed said she wanted her man to make her feel like a woman.

To that I asked, "What makes you feel like a woman?"

"Ah, there's that look of appreciation that says he's enjoying being with me. I like that appreciation."

* * * * * *

Since many of us are tempted to risk being dishonest at one time or another with the woman in our life, I asked:

If you discovered that your man had lied to you, what would be your reaction?

THE ANSWER I GOT MOST OFTEN was, "I'd confront him." That response was immediate and invariably given without thought. They followed with, "I'd want to know why he lied." Their reason for wanting to know why the lie, was so they could decide between

dumping him or sticking around. The CPA secretary explained:
"I would want to know why he found it necessary to lie. His lying makes me feel bad about myself... what may I have done wrong? Am I such an ogre that he is afraid to tell me the truth? If that's so, then I feel partly to blame and would search within myself to see if I need to change. At the same time, his lying would strain my respect for him."

A blonde twenty-seven-year-old television personality answered, "If he lied over something extremely important to me, like a lie to cover unfaithfulness, he'd be history. Not because of jealousy ... I would just be embarrassed as hell."

And this from a professional counselor: "I'd examine our whole relationship. A romantic relationship between two people is a family system. If there's something unhealthy within that system ... for instance, if my expectations are too difficult for him to meet, he might be pushed into a lie. Before blaming him, I need to look at the whole relationship. I need to know why he felt he couldn't tell me the truth. After that, we can either solve the problem, which would improve our relationship, fix blame, or split."

The wife of a general contractor said of being lied to: "That lousy SOB. If he thinks I can't take the truth, what does he think I'm made of'?" She smiled. "I caught him in only one lie during our marriage. He said he was late because the foursome ahead was slow. Later I found out he had been somewhere else and lied about it. When I confronted him, during the discussion he said, 'You're damned right I have a double standard ... one for you and one for me.' So I said, 'Okay, now we both know the rules.'" She chuckled. "I guess the twinkle in my eye scared him because, as far as I know, he never lied to me again. When he died, a lot of people told me they admired my husband because you knew where you stood with him, you didn't have to guess about it. The truth is the only way."

Another professional counselor said of lying, "Many women don't want to know if their husband is fooling around. These women view a lie as protecting their feelings. Problem is, they don't know if he had a one-time fling, or if he is seeing the other woman regularly. If it's regular, the wife is kidding herself about a lie to protect her. She's got her head in the sand."

A twenty-year-old cosmetologist said, "When I caught him, I'd scream and yell. Then I'd look for the reason behind his lie, and why it was more important for him to lie than tell the truth. Finally, whether I stayed around or not would depend on what he had lied about. If it was another woman, while I packed I would wish him good luck with her."

A twenty-nine-year-old paralegal said, "Confront him. If he lied about another woman in his life ... change that to *our* life ... I'd probably sever the relationship. If he lied about spending too much money on something, we'd work that out."

A twenty-seven-year-old bank teller stated, "I'd be hurt and angry, but I'd want to know the reason. If he was afraid or ashamed of whatever he lied about, that's no problem, so long as he takes steps to cure those problems. But if he isn't willing to improve himself toward being truthful with me in the future, I'd eventually terminate the relationship."

A thirty-one-year-old graduate student mused, "I'd pretend I didn't know he lied, and then would lay plans to catch him in the act. I might set him up with leading questions that give him a chance to either be truthful or deceitful. His answers would tell me how he intends to deal with me in the future. If he isn't truthful, I'm outta' there."

One woman snapped, "The first time he lied to me would be his last."

A thirty-seven-year-old animal behaviorist swore, "I'd feel like punching his lights out. I also believe that what's good for the goose is good for the gander. He's gonna know that if he lies to me, he may get lied to."

A thirty-three-year-old camera repair technician and photographer answered, "I'd be angry first. Then I'd want to know the reason. I don't care what the reason turns out to be ... just be straight with me. The truth happened. It is real. A lie is fiction ... don't convert truth into fiction."

A forty-one-year-old accountant said, "I'd be hurt, resentful, and unforgiving. That he found a need to lie, no matter how trivial, would be almost impossible for me to forget. From then on, I would be no good to him, so he may as well leave."

Often I heard women wonder what *they* were doing that would cause a man not to be truthful. I asked one lady her opinion of that stance.

Her answer was: "Bullcorn. There's no way I'm going to take the blame for his lying. It's his problem to solve, not mine. If he lies to me, he lies to me on his own two feet, not mine. I'm not taking the blame for his shortcomings."

A thirty-seven-year-old published author observed, "In a healthy relationship, there's no need to lie."

A forty-five-year-old cattle rancher said, "When I'm lied to and make decisions on those lies, I look stupid. I don't like to look stupid. Since I can only make intelligent decisions on facts, I'd withdraw from a relationship that included lies."

Notice that "confront him" was a universal, often instant response to the question of being lied to by a man. The women's feelings were, in general, that men tend to avoid confrontation. They considered men's proclivity to avoid situations that are uncomfortable to them as a male weakness. Obviously women have strong feelings about being lied to, especially about another woman. However, in other lies these wonderful women seemed fair-minded enough to "work it out" and then fit a punishment to match the crime.

* * * * * *

The women had other elements on their wish list of what they want from men, including "good sex" (see pages 78-126). But since simply getting along with women ranks high in many men's minds, the next question I asked each woman was:

When men and women don't get along smoothly, in your opinion, what are the primary causes of conflict?

A THIRTY-ONE-YEAR-OLD MOTEL DESK CLERK laughed and snapped, "Men and women don't get along because women tend to think with their hearts while men tend to think from below the belt, with their wallets and their peckers."

After we stopped laughing, she added, "Seriously, poor communication probably causes most of the conflict between men and women."

Fifty-two percent of the women agreed with the clerk's premise. To those women, I asked, "Who do you think is poorest at communication, men or women?"

Thirty-eight of the fifty-two women who believed communication was a central problem said they thought men in general had poorer verbal skills than women. A forty-six-year-old marriage counselor explained, "As girls grow up, they tend to gather in small groups and talk, talk, talk. While the girls are learning to talk, the boys are playing king of the hill, or football, basketball, baseball, etc. So boys learn to grunt and shout, while girls learn to converse." She lifted her arms in an emphatic shrug. "Why should we be surprised that men aren't as good at conversation as women?" She leaned toward me and shook her finger. "But wait a minute, guys ... that's an excuse for only so long. Effective communication can be learned," she beamed. "Look at the list of male writers, poets, journalists, lawyers, and so on, who *have learned* to communicate ... often with a skill beyond a lot of women."

The marriage counselor went on to say she thought that when men make the effort, they learn to converse as well, or better, than women. She added, "I think men *know* their true feelings ... they just haven't been given either role modeling or motive to learn how to verbalize those feelings. To make matters worse, women often say to their man, 'Tell me what you're feeling,' when what she's really saying is, 'Please tell me ... talk to me. I may have an answer to your problem.'"

She continued. "Unfortunately, men don't easily pick up on indirect approaches. Why should they? Their serious conversations have often been no more than 'shoot' on the basketball court, 'go' from the third base line, and, from king of the hill, nothing more than grunt and shove. Their long conversations have been 'great shot,' 'way to go,' and 'hang in there.' Many men haven't equipped themselves to deal with the words necessary to carry on a conversation, *or* they talk in circles."

I asked, "Okay, but why do women circle the mulberry bush when talking with a man?"

"Women circle the bush because they realize a man's ego is fragile in a one-on-one conversation." She laughed. "Funny ... we don't want to injure a man's ego, yet we expect him, unfairly, to be a mind reader."

She continued: "Unfortunately, men have compensated by noticing that a 'right' answer is expected, so they join her dance around the bush, looking for, 'What does she want me to say?' rather than saying what's really on their minds. Often the man knows what he wants to say, but won't risk saying it. From my experience, he'd like to say, 'I don't know what I'm feeling' or 'this is too big' or 'I don't know how to handle it right now.' But the thought of saying those things, at the expense of appearing 'unmacho' scares him." She raised her hands aloft. "All this bush circling and expected mind reading could be eliminated if men would simply learn the basics of conversation. For one thing, men would learn, as women have, that words often will solve problems ... words will show the way. Most men don't seem to understand that."

She paused. "The problem is, either men have not been taught, or they simply have not learned on their own, to communicate with words as well as women. Therefore, men haven't learned to trust words in social intercourse or problem solving." She chuckled. "Men may not be as good at words as women; however, they can be absolutely effective at communicating without words."

She laughed, and added, "There is little that is more effective than, in the middle of a discussion, puffing up and walking out of the room."

She continued. "Many women are hurt and confused by puff-and-walk, because suddenly their words aren't aces anymore ... remember, we believe, with good reason, that words can solve most everything. Other wordless communications that men tend to use are slamming a door, or not coming home, and so on. Those forms of communicating strain a woman's patience. Also, she feels threatened, because a slamming door reduces her opportunity to resolve the problem in a mutually beneficial way."

Another point this counselor made was, "Each of us is always communicating. Unfortunately, often what some people say to one who tries to establish verbal contact is, 'Get out of my face ... I don't want to hear what you're saying.'" She paused, and then added: "Guys, you might be surprised at the rewards that can come from a woman when you let her know, 'Hey, I want you in my face ... I want to see you, and I want you to see me, so that between your ideas and mine, we may solve problems, and create a more pleasant life for both of us.'"

A service manager in a defense plant gave her impression of man/woman communication: "I think men have too many conversational taboos, because, for whatever reason, they perceive some subjects as not manly. They cover up by trying to be macho. They're too guarded ... trying to keep you from seeing the real them. Not seeing the inner man destroys any chance for intimacy (see page 59). I crave the intimacy that can *only* come from knowing the whole person. It's a strong man who will share his inner self. Younger men seem more open to conversation ... to talking about everything, including what they think is manly and what's not. Older men seem to have a tougher time relearning that any subject should be okay.... . So-called manly has nothing to do with it."

I learned how freely women will talk with a man about *anything* when I asked how they felt about oral sex (see page 102).

A twenty-eight-year-old said, "The problem is, men would rather talk to a group of buddies than one-on-one with their woman. I think that has to do with men's egos ... they seem afraid to express their feelings because it might show some sensitive side, a side many men are afraid to show for fear of becoming vulnerable."

"Would you consider a man weak, or un-macho if he shared his feelings?" I enquired.

Emphatically she shook her head. "Never. Men, please don't be afraid to talk to us openly. You'd be surprised at how endearing, even sexy, a so-called weakness can be to a woman."

A red-haired secretary explained how she prefers communication with a male: "Pay attention to us ... listen to us. We aren't all stupid, as some of you seem to think. Interact with your female partner and try to be more sensitive to her (emotional) needs, for example, when I am making love and communicate my sexual needs to a man—to me, penetration may not be that important. He can arouse and please me in other ways. For example, his hands and mouth can be more satisfying to me than aiming his penis my direction. But to pick up on my needs, he must 'hear' me. And if he's really good, way before the trip to bed, he can arouse me mentally by talking with me about things that I am, or he is, interested in. Such talk may take place across hours ... and no sexual innuendoes, please. The level of talk I want takes time. If he is willing to take that time, it suggests he is a man somewhere above wham-bam. If he listens, and pays attention to my emotional needs first and foremost, he reaches a point where he becomes irresistible. In other words, if he isn't interested in me enough to connect with my mind, don't bother trying to connect with my body."

I asked a twenty-eight-year-old television news camerawoman her opinion as to where man/woman communications lay, and where we are headed.

"Since the 70s, role barriers have been broken, and we've all been kinda stuck out there not knowing exactly what the new boundaries are. To me it's created a lot of friction. For men, I think it has been more devastating, because they were raised to be 'a man,' and a man is supposed to be head of the house, and do manly things. I appreciate it if a man will share in responsibilities that used to be considered female, because I'm out there (in the work place) doing what he normally did. Now I will not give up that lifestyle of independence that working provides. I'm too independent to back up and give that over to a man."

When I asked, "Do you think women are on the cutting edge of breaking old molds and men are slower to adapt?" the camerawoman replied:

"I think so. A lot of men seem more lost than the women are. Women are survivors ... we have to be because we are the childbearers. We're forced into survival, whereas men are kinda out there bumping into walls, asking themselves, 'If I'm not this role, what am I?' He's wondering that since he's supposed to be Mr. Macho and Mr. Everything, what is he when a woman not only takes some of that away from him, but also asks for help in 'female' chores? New women are creating a lot of insecurity in some men."

"Do you think men will ever adapt?" I asked.

"I think they have to. It's not going to be easy. I think male egos are so out of proportion, it's going to be real hard for them. When some of them are asked to help around the house, they're probably going to stiffen and go 'Say hey?' It's like our Native American Indians ... when they didn't have a place and a touchstone, they got real lost. It takes a long time to evolve into a different position. Changing is going to be tough on the male population. Men learning to communicate is the answer."

An example of problems that are created by lack of good communication is a sad/funny story from a bright, articulate, attractive forty-four-year-old Texan. This woman had a passion for dancing that she traced to childhood dreams of becoming a ballerina. In the nineteen years they were married, her husband not only never took her dancing, he also made it clear that he never would. The dancing issue remained unresolved for the life of their marriage. The woman believed that this problem eroded their communication, which contributed to their eventual split. (She lamented that he never once told her how he felt about her.)

After their divorce, during a test of her former husband's hearing, it was discovered that he was musically and rhythmically deaf. Communication might have resolved their problem.

Here are other comments women had about communication:

A brunette comptroller for a heavy equipment firm said, "To look me in the eye and talk to me, *openly*, is to touch my mind. If you can't touch my mind, you cannot touch my body."

A blonde newspaper reporter summed up her feeling about communication: "Hey guys, you'd be surprised at how much more valuable a female companion can be if you will deal more with her head on a continuing basis ... not just to con her for your short term pleasure. You may con her for a while, but she'll catch on (women are smart, remember?) and when she does, you're history."

A thirty-eight-year-old lawyer said, "I think men sometimes don't 'talk about it' because they don't want to rock the boat ... that's how men avoid conflict. Besides, they think, or *hope*, things will work out on their own if given enough time. Well, while she waits for him to say something about the problem, not only does it not go away, often it grows bigger." She looked me in the eye. "This may surprise you, but when a problem grows, some women celebrate."

Celebrate? I'm sure my eyebrows jumped at this revelation.

She smiled. "Some women like to keep a relationship on edge. To do that, she either creates a problem, or contentedly watches a small, insignificant one grow."

I've heard stories about female mysteriousness, or contrariness, driving men to distraction. It appeared that what the lawyer was saying might be shining light into a dark corner of a woman's mind. Feeling I was on to something, I cautiously asked, "Why would a woman want to keep a relationship on edge?"

The lawyer shifted in her chair. "Problems add excitement to her life, so she makes something happen ... anything, partly because when women co-workers ask 'What did you do last night?' to answer 'nothing' is embarrassing." She grinned. "To be certain of having something to talk about, these women keep their man on edge and then gleefully retell, blow by blow, the fight they had last night."

She looked out a window, as if not sure she should let me look into this side of the female brain. Quietly, I waited. She continued to look away and finished with, "And the fight is usually about dumb little things ... which TV show to watch ... what movie to go to." She glanced at me and almost sheepishly added, "She may have also learned that when she puts him on edge, he may defensively fall back on telling her he loves her, or that she's beautiful. He probably says these things while he's trying to figure out 'what's going on here?'" She looked away again. "Tension can also increase her need for sexual release."

Her candor may explain a few male/female conflicts I have witnessed wherein I wondered, "Why?" Until this interview, I tended to credit those strange arguments to a woman's right to change her mind or to blame PMS. Apparently, deliberate tactics may be more common than we suspect. Two other women I interviewed said they used manufactured conflicts to "keep him off balance." Another admitted that manufactured conflicts at least gained his attention. She pointed out that when she was attention starved, even the wrong kind was better than nothing.

Apparently these women are a small minority of the female population (only three percent of the number I inter viewed). Even so, I wished I'd known about the phenomenon when I was eighteen. I was feeling smug at my newly-gained information when the lawyer shifted her posture, crossed her legs, and made circles in the air with her foot. "Have you ever wondered why some women seem to prefer going after married men?"

"I hadn't given it thought, but I'm interested in your ideas."

"The so-called 'other woman' has an inherent advantage over a married man. She can push him all over the board."

Now consider a different, possibly positive, outcome that may result from male/female conflict. A forty-four-year-old high school teacher said, "I have friends who seem to keep their relationship good by fighting." She laughed. "It's interesting when you think about the relationships of friends, for example, couples that fight often. On the surface, you'd think their relationship was in difficulty. When they air their laundry in screaming matches, we automatically think they might be in trouble."

A serious look came on her face. "But in the long run, these couples often have a more stable relationship than couples who appear to get along smoothly. So often the smooth ones shock us when they up and get a divorce." She smiled. "Maybe those smooth couples are really just smoldering along, smoldering because they don't have that vehicle of conflict. (After all, conflict can be a means of communication … the idea being, get him into a conflict, and you have him communicating!) Those couples who seem to be in deep trouble are able to thrash differences out, and things get resolved.

"Ventilating problems may help get solutions that keep a couple together." She looked pensive. "But then maybe they're the ones who know how to fight fairly … without getting personal or negative. Maybe they're the ones who know the art of communication."

Here is how a fifty-five-year-old homemaker solved communication problems with her husband. She admits she is the one who had to learn to communicate. "In the beginning of my marriage, I didn't want to hurt his feelings. I loved him dearly, so I kept things in. In the first year or two it was difficult for us to communicate, because I kept upsets to myself. Sometimes I wrote them down, thinking it would be less painful if I wrote them in a letter. Eventually I realized that if my marriage was going to survive, I had to learn to communicate more effectively. He made it easier because he wasn't bashful about telling me things he didn't like ... he didn't seem to worry about hurting my feelings, yet I knew he loved me. So I decided, what the heck, I was going to do the same. I decided just to be open with him, and let the chips fall. So one day I laid out to him what I wanted discussed, and cussed. It helped that he was already good with words. Sure enough, we got over little problems before they became big. Thirty-five years later, we have a strong, loving relationship that grows stronger with each problem solved. I credit our success to my not holding it in, and learning to be open with him about my true feelings."

A thirty-eight-year-old high school speech and English teacher echoed the foregoing comments about man/woman communication problems. Then she said, "In this day and age, there's no excuse for remaining poor at communication. There are good books on the subject ... one I can think of is a small paperback, *The Art of Conversation* by James Morris (Prentice Hall, 1978)."

It appears the women have lobbed the conversational ball into our court. Our challenge seems to be to learn how to keep the ball in play.

Next to poor communication, *power struggles* were defined as the second major cause (at fifteen percent) of conflicts between men and women. Some of the women's observations were: "If one is raised having things his/her way, a person isn't likely to give in to another, and there comes trouble. If you learn young to give and take, then give and take is easier as an adult."

Another woman said, "Each wants to be boss ... one wants to dominate, and that's a power struggle. I think women fight for power more than men."

A radio sales representative said, "In general, I think men downplay women to 'keep women in their place.' For example, the men I work with are competent and aggressive in the business world, yet when the office coffee pot is dry they become helpless. I think that's a power play, and I resent it."

A power company publicist put it this way: "Some men were raised to believe 'I-am-the-man-therefore-I-shall-be-obeyed.' A little of that causes some women to react with, 'Don't-order-me-around-and-why-do-I-have-to-ask-your-permission?' More often than not, this kind of man allows the woman to make the insignificant decisions ... according to him, that's 'woman's department.' The important decision department he takes for himself."

"And you have trouble with that?" I prompted.

"You bet your boots I do. It's why he's there and I'm here."

A thirty-five-year-old author and speaker had suggestions for reducing, and possibly eliminating, power struggles. She pointed out that, "Many of us were raised to get what we want out of life by using a 'win/lose' mentality. That means we think that to get what we want, you must lose, or at least be hurt. That attitude comes from some childhood authority relationships. A few parents and teachers taught us by their example that because they were bigger, they could hurt us if we didn't do what they demanded. That's using power for control and a poor model for teaching how to get what we want. When we take that attitude into a relationship, it is bound to breed conflict, because one person is considering only their needs, with no regard for the other's. One or the other believes, 'Well, I have to show him/her who is boss ... I can't let him/her push me around.' In that atmosphere, original goals get lost in the power struggle. Win/lose turns into push/shove. A less damaging way is for each partner to ask him/herself, 'How can I get what I want, and at the same time see that you get what you want?' Put another way, 'How can I get what I want without depriving or hurting you?' That way we both win." She took a breath. "Another damaging event to communication is when one or the other has something to hide. Even when he or she is skillful at communicating, exchanges become fewer and fewer for fear of making a slip. At that point the relationship begins to suffer. Cutting lines of communication is a sure way to murder a relationship, and cutting communication is sometimes used as a weapon to do just that."

The thirty-nine-year-old wife of a doctor described power struggles as, "where the lady wants to have the final say, and so does the guy. It goes back to yours, mine, and ours. If you have separate bank accounts, you're in a power struggle (and probably in trouble). I think it has to be all ours, with everything going into a family kitty. The more they operate as two single entities, the less there is to the relationship. For one thing, not pooling financial resources says, 'I don't trust you.' My grandmother ... a very wise lady ... said, 'If you put him first, and he puts you first, there is no power struggle.'" The doctor's wife looked wistful. "My grandmother was beautifully married for almost eighty years."

Other causes of conflict that concerned the one hundred women were:

Money differences, 14%
Having too many expectations
    (on the part of one or the other) 6%
Differences in interests, 5%
Differences in sexual ideas, 3%
Inconsideration, 2%
Lack of intimacy, 2%
Having out-of-shape egos, 1%
Having nothing in common 1%
Inflexibility, 1%
Lack of commitment, 1%
Insensitivity, 1%.

I asked the professional counselor what *her* experience revealed as the greatest cause of conflict between men and women. "Invariably the issue is, 'Are you taking care of me the way I want to be taken care of?' That's the number one area of conflict that is brought for me to referee." She explained, "Taking care of includes communicating ... listening ... talking ... and house cleaning, cooking, sex, money, and so on ... whatever areas that are important to each. The big question in any or all of these is, 'Are you taking care of me the way I want to be taken care of?'"

That question/statement struck me as a gold-plated observation.

* * * * * *

Since women who like themselves seem more pleasant to be with, I asked them:

What can a man do that makes you feel good about yourself?

THE ANSWER FROM a fifty-year-old widow echoed how woman after woman answered: "Women need ... it's probably born in them ... approval. They need it in everything. That's why we take so much care to dress and put all this makeup on. We do it because we need approval, a compliment, or acknowledgment that I'm here and cared for by someone. That caring is one of the things I look for. I want someone who really gives a damn about whether I am or not. If he notices me, that says he cares. If he doesn't notice me, I get the idea he either doesn't care, or he is mentally reducing me to an invisible ... a non-person. A little of that, and I'll be invisible alright... ."

"Compliment me" was the answer I heard over and over again. Here are examples: "Small compliments ... in any area. The way I've fixed the house; my clothes; my makeup; be alert to what I'm doing. Notice. Any kind of compliment."

The cosmetologist had the following request: "Don't give me empty compliments such as 'You have a nice body,' or 'How come you're so pretty.' I like being complemented about something I have control over, such as my personality. If somebody thinks I'm funny, or enjoyable to be with, or smart, or thoughtful ... those are the kinds of things that make me feel like I'm not interchangeable with some other beautiful body. It's as if any person with a nice body could fill that slot. A compliment like that makes me feel that in his mind, if he found someone with a nicer body, I might be history. That makes me uncomfortable ... like I was a cow being judged."

I inquired, "Is how you dress important for you to hear?"

"Not particularly. I like how I dress, so I'm not insecure about that. The main thing I'm interested in is where our relationship is ... information about that. If he tells me he enjoys being with me, that makes me feel good."

"Compliment me on how competent I am. Like, 'Gee, that was a really successful party we had,' or 'That was a nice trip, and I had a good time with you,' or 'That was a great piece of work you did.'"

A brunette said, "I think a lot of men have a fear of complimenting their partner because they feel that isn't macho ... they feel like they may be vulnerable. To me, that man is either weak or stupid."

An office worker said, "I'm complimented when a man asks me to do something, such as form a committee for some project he has in mind. Or, if a man asks my opinion on something, I take that as a personal compliment. He has given me freedom to put together a project, which says he recognizes my ability to do a specific job. When he asks my opinion, that says he values my ideas. That makes me feel very good about myself, and makes me feel I'm of value to him."

A housewife said, "He makes me feel good about myself if

he notices little things I've done, notices my hair if it's different, or a new dress. That says he senses I'm there ... that I'm not being ignored. Or if I've spent time fixing a meal for him, and then he tells me he appreciates what I've done, it's important that he tells me if it was good or if it was bad. That doesn't bother me at all, so long as he recognizes the effort I've made. Those things mean more to me than a gift."

A Santa Fe shop owner said, "I feel good in myself if the man is confident in his lifestyle. If his lifestyle is insecure, paranoid, guilty, and jealous, then after a while, I get that way too, and the relationship gets real sick. But if he is confident and secure, I feel those energies too, and they become shared. In other words, if he is basically negative, in time, I will feel negative. But if he feels up, so do I. Mind you, if it's a passing kind of negative, I ride through it feeling okay. But if it's an inherent behavior and lifestyle, I don't want that, and I'm gonna' be out of there, because a constant negative attitude will eventually bring me down. I can only be so strong for so long and try to pretend like something is going to change. If it doesn't, I begin to feel bad about myself. Since I don't need that, I'll soon be gone, looking for a more positive, good feeling."

Other areas besides compliments that make a woman feel good about herself were:

"I like romance. Guys who have won me bring out big brooms and start sweeping. I've had some that kept sweeping throughout the relationship ... while others, once they had me, put the broom down. I love flowers. Getting flowers from a guy shows respect, admiration, and a little something extra. Flowers make me feel special."

The television camera person said, "The best compliment I can get is for a man to read me ... tell by my eyes, or by the way I walk, or the tone of my voice, that I've had a bad day. He makes me feel great if he picks up on that, and then fixes me by insisting I sit down and relax, while he starts the meal, or finishes the laundry, or whatever. That man gets my heart."

This woman said she wanted her man to "tell me how I look. I want to hear how I look, good or bad. Just don't ignore me."

The public service parts woman said, "I have concluded that I'm a workaholic because I get all my strokes at work. People tell me I'm doing a great job, that I'm helping build a wonderful business, etc. When I go home it's, 'When is dinner going to be ready?' or 'Why aren't the dishes washed?' I think men miss the boat by not giving their woman enough strokes at home."

The female lawyer said, "A man makes me feel good when he gives me a true compliment. To tell me I handled that case well gives me a glow. But I don't like manufactured compliments. I don't want someone to compliment just to make points. I want compliments more about my accomplishments than about something I'm wearing or how I look. Anyone can buy a pretty outfit and, in a way, 'buy a compliment.' Maybe this is why some women just go shopping and splurge on a new outfit. Maybe if their man gave them an honest compliment about something they did, there would be no need to go out and spend money on what often turns out to be frivolous, temporary, feel-good items. The other side of that coin is, she must do something worthwhile ... cook ... housekeep ... sew ... child-rear ... career achievement ... something worth complimenting. If she's a couch potato, she isn't likely to draw many compliments."

The television reporter said, "I want physical affection that isn't always tied to sex. Holding hands, or a kiss as he walks by me in the house. Also, I wish he would look at me like he thought I was important ... somebody more than just a body. Make me feel loved without saying, 'Okay, I made you feel loved, now let's get it on.' I want genuine affection. Otherwise I feel the only time he tells me he loves me is when he wants to take me to bed. That doesn't cut it. I feel used, like I'm an object."

* * * * * *

I tried to pace my questions in a way that helped each woman feel at ease. My next question was done in that light:

What is your idea of an enjoyable way to spend time, such as an afternoon or evening, with a man?

AN ADDITIONAL MOTIVE for this question was to reduce the guesswork on a man's part as to what a woman might like to do on a date. I was surprised and believe you will be too, at how the majority of women answered.

The answer I heard most often (fifty-five percent) was, "A walk, in the park." At first, I simply ran a tally on the variety of answers. At that time I didn't ask why a particular activity rated high for spending time with a man. My education came when a young male co-worker, who knew I was interviewing women, asked what kind of questions I asked. As an example, I gave him the above question, and told him the answer I was hearing the most.

A couple of weeks later he caught me in the break room, said he had tried that walk in the park with his girlfriend, and it didn't work ... whatever "didn't work" implied. Curious, I asked him to recount his experience.

The young man said they were getting along fine, until he began giving her photographic lessons on his camera. "That ended our walk in the park," he said.

Mystified, I pondered his experience. It took a couple of days to figure out why his walk in the park with his girlfriend ended so abruptly. (Some of you already know the answer and are racing ahead of my words. If you're chuckling at my—and his—slowness, please don't be too harsh. We men can be slow at times.) Gradually it dawned on me that the appeal to a woman for a walk in the park with her man is, she has his full attention: no phones, no children, no neighbors, no camera, no distractions. In the park or on a picnic, it is her and him ... one on one, which is what she wants. To verify my thoughts, in subsequent interviews I followed up with, "Why a walk in the park?" Woman after woman confirmed my "brilliant" deduction.

Later I asked the young man's girlfriend why his camera instructions, at that moment, were such a turn off. She answered, "It made me feel uninteresting, unlovable, and unattractive. Previous times, with other friends who didn't bring a distraction, were good and satisfying. Those good times haunted me and I wanted more. I wanted him to address me one hundred percent."

Another side of that coin, however, could be a red flag that a man needs to consider. When I told the above story to another woman, she made this point: "Camera instructions would have been fine with me. That would have said he cared enough about me to include me in his world. Since she was put off by his camera, that may indicate she wasn't really that interested in him, or his world. It may also say she has no interest in learning anything new. Her put-off could also be a clue that she is self-centered, caring only about things she cares about. If his interests bother her, that may show that she wants one hundred percent of his attention, all the time. If I were this guy, I'd run."

After hearing those opinions, I carried my question one step further and asked, "How much one-on-one time do you want with your man?" Answers varied from "one hundred percent" to "five minutes once a week." Since the amount of pure time a woman wants from her man varied so much from individual to individual, it may be important to establish that information on an individual basis. What a woman may expect of your undivided attention might be more than you are willing to give.

Other ways the ladies wished to spend time with their man were:

Dinner, at home or out, 20%
Movie, 5% (sometimes combined with dinner)
Theater, 3%
Dancing, 2%
Home together, 2%
Art gallery or museum, 2%
Golf, 2%
Share in a mutual interest, 2%
Bicycle ride, 1%
Boating, 1%
Camping, 1%
By the fireplace, 1%
Game of pool, 1%
Tennis, 1%
Afternoon in bed, 1%
Spectator sport, 1%
Zoo, 1%

Here are comments individual women made about spending time with their man. A forty-four-year-old advertising agency owner said, "I'm a romantic. I like to take a picnic basket to the park. That's my idea of a perfect afternoon. I'd like to have an hour of uninterrupted time just to communicate. If it's evening, a candle-lit bedroom, with soft music and wine, and let nature run."

"How often do you want that kind of time?" I asked.

"Not more than once a week. I'm raising two teenage boys and run a business. If I could have a Saturday or Sunday afternoon, or one night a week, it would fill my bucket. I couldn't handle seven days a week. And I don't want this time to be scheduled, but spontaneous. I don't want sex to be scheduled, either."

A forty-three-year-old brunette radio salesperson, with an IQ giving her membership in MENSA, said, "One of the most enjoyable evenings I've ever had was a walk in the park. We were both attending a broadcast convention. He asked me to walk with him because he didn't have money enough to take us anywhere. We couldn't even afford brunch following a morning business meeting. That walk in the park with him was a most enjoyable time for me ... a standout."

A forty-eight-year-old bank executive secretary stated, "How I want to spend time with him would depend on my mood. I'm about five women in one. Most likely I'd like to rent three movies, lock the door, close the curtains, and lie back with him. Or, I might want a candlelight dinner. Then I can have his time and attention. He used to think being romantic was frivolous, sissified. Now he finds quality time important. He learned to be a romantic from me." She laughed. "It shows men can be taught... they can learn. I love him to death for it."

A thirty-three-year-old camera repair technician said she wanted her quality time to be outdoors in the daytime. Her theory was, "Always go on three daytime dates first. On daytime dates, there's less worry about sexual stuff ... you avoid that late evening decision of what do I do if he asks me to sleep with him, before I really have a chance to know him. I think women lean toward outdoor activities because that takes the sexual pressure off. Sex can kill you now. It's hard to be single in today's world."

A fifty-year-old teacher said, "The thing about walking in nature is that you're looking out for yourself, and so much more can go through your mind. At dinner, conversation can get stuck on talking about the same things ... unless the person has a mind that slips around easily. But when you're walking in the outdoors, there are built-in silences, such as when you're getting through a fence, or crossing a stream. I find that walking among the trees with someone allows me to see the real person, rather than seeing him as a salesman, or engineer, or pilot. And walks in the woods invariably turn up surprises. I like that sense of mutual discovery.

"It gives me a chance to see if he is turned on by a bed of wildflowers, or whatever. Surprise is the key ingredient for me on a date. I like things to be unpredictable. I like a man who says, 'Hey, I want to take you to such and such.' It's hard when he asks, 'What do you want to do?' I prefer he take the lead, surprise me with something he views as special and different."

Another lady I interviewed likes surprises. This forty-one-year-old accountant said, "I love to be surprised. It would be wonderful if he would plan something ... take charge and go with it, and let me be totally passive. I love that."

One thirty-eight-year-old escrow officer in a title company

said of dinner at home, "I want us to prepare the meal together. Then we can both take credit for a great meal, or if it's bad, we can share the blame."

Miscellaneous comments from some of the women were, "Most of us are so involved, we don't have to be entertained to have an enjoyable evening. I enjoy nightgowns and slippers and popping corn watching a good TV show. It doesn't take a big production for me to have an enjoyable evening."

"I don't have to be wined and dined. That's plastic. Sometimes it's okay, but what really matters is what comes from his heart and his eyes ... not his credit cards."

* * * * * *

My next question was designed to help prevent men from blundering into getting crossways with a woman. The question was:

What can a man do that annoys you or makes you uncomfortable?

MOST OFTEN I HEARD, "Put me down." For a glimpse of how put downs affected one woman, hear this pretty forty-four-year-old mother of three and holder of two college degrees. She was one of the brightest, wittiest, most beautiful women I've ever met. She said, "For fifteen years my husband put me down ... told me I was stupid, no good, and ugly."

"But you're the opposite of ugly," I remarked. "In fact, you're a striking beauty."

She lowered her head. "No I'm not."

"You said you're divorced. Why continue parroting him?"

"I have this little block in here that says he told me I wasn't pretty, so I'm not."

"Then look in the mirror."

"I do, but it makes no difference. It's what he said that counts."

As I watched this woman, I was saddened that a man had such an impact on her mind. The thought occurred that he might make a good cult leader.

A twenty-six-year-old telephone repair person said of being put down, "I'm open to having things explained to me; I'm eager to learn new things, and I can make mistakes. But don't talk down to me as if I can't do any of the above. I get the feeling sometimes that he thinks no more of my ideas than he would a dog's."

A twenty-nine-year-old radio PR person and promotion writer said, "Some of my dates let me know that because they are a man, they understand about such and such ... insinuating that because I'm a woman, I don't or can't understand such and such as well as he does. Or he'll say, 'Here, let me do that, because you can't do it right.' He may as well have said, 'Dummy, get out of the way.' I hate that."

The second most common complaint about what a man does that annoys women was, "Not communicating." Examples were: "They don't listen. I think they hear, but they aren't listening. When we say something to them, too often they mechanically say 'okay' as a way of dismissing us and getting on with whatever it is they are doing. It's as if a woman's voice is an interruption to their lives."

A thirty-four-year-old housewife said, "When he doesn't communicate, that annoys me. When he won't tell me what's worrying or bothering him I can't read his mind, and I don't want to play twenty questions."

A teacher and bookstore owner said, "I'm annoyed when he doesn't talk or show any expression in his face when he does. Either of those says to me that he doesn't like me. The man I was dating lived a pretty expressionless life, and he had no character wrinkles in his face. Sometimes I scrunched his face up to give it character and meaning. He was wearisome. I'm more comfortable with men who talk a lot ... and who have character wrinkles."

The third ranked complaint was from working women who wanted at least a fifty-fifty split on housekeeping duties.

Other complaints were:

The financial counselor said, "Not listening to me, or shutting me off when I'm trying to talk to somebody. Also, invalidating my feelings when I'm upset about something. If I'm upset, I don't want to hear that what I'm upset about is ridiculous. I want somebody to at least try and understand. Also, it annoys me if he's going to be late and doesn't call. No problem if he calls ... I'll just reset my brain and go on about my business."

Other comments were:

"Not to give me his undivided attention when we're talking ... a stray eye, looking around to see who is coming in the door, or who's leaving. When I talk with a man, I want eye contact."

"I hate it when he's talking to me, but looking at some other woman."

"When he looks at other women, that annoys me. And as I

get a little older I dislike that even more. In the mall when we pass some sweet young thing without a wrinkle, I'm pissed when his eyes glue to her and his head swivels. And I don't want to hear oohs and aahs when some sweet thing pops on TV. I don't ooh and ah at some young handsome dude in the mall or on TV, because I respect my man's feelings."

Miscellaneous annoyances were: "Doesn't listen and interrupts. When he interrupts, he's obviously not listening."

"I hate it when a man gets real particular with the waitress ... complaining or asking for items that aren't necessary. That's more a show of power, and it's a turn off."

"When he tells me what he thinks I'm thinking, rather than asking me. Like if I'm sad and he says, 'You're not, either.' Or he asks me something and I tell him, and then he says that what I answered is not really what I think. If that's the way he feels, why bother to ask? Did he think I got up this morning to lie to him?"

"I'm uncomfortable with the cocky bodybuilder who reeks with, 'Aren't I wonderful, and macho, neat?' And I'm going *ugh*. They're a real turn off."

To this, I asked, "Why? I thought women were attracted to hunks."

"Being toned and physically fit is one thing, but the attitude that 'I have to be the most muscular, the biggest, and the brawniest' is immature. When they reach the point where they say, 'Sorry dear ... can't talk ... gotta go press benches,' that's selfishness, and beyond being a hunk."

When I asked an executive secretary what men do that annoyed her she said, "The top of my list is the macho thing. To me he's saying, 'I'm not real sure who I am, so I'm going to prove I'm a man through macho posturing.' That usually means domination. Too often the macho bunch thinks I'm supposed to accept as fact that male gender has license to dominate. An example is when more importance is given to the birth of a boy than a girl. That's where it starts." She smiled. "Even male horses are treated as more important. When a male horse is born, we have a horse. But when a female horse is born, we have a filly, as if a filly isn't a horse."

The motel night clerk made a soapbox speech about things men do that make her uncomfortable. At times, her thoughts went beyond the scope of the question. Nevertheless, I felt she had ideas that were valuable to a man wanting to start a relationship with a woman, or a man wanting to maintain a relationship. Therefore, I present her ideas in their entirety. By way of review, the question was, "What can a man do that annoys you or makes you feel uncomfortable?" Her answer was:

"To be plastic or phony. His trying to make me believe he is something he's not. To be phony at presenting himself as gallant, mannerly, chivalrous."

I asked, "Do you find these qualities more often phony than genuine?"

"Yes. Men tend to be a lot like women, more so than ten to twenty years ago. Women can really be phony and plastic ... we let you see only what we want you to see. In recent years, men have gotten more like that. Ten to twenty years ago they were more down to earth. Then men's attitudes seemed to be, 'This is what I am, take me or leave me.' I think society is forcing men to be a little more polished, to a point that they are a little more phony."

"Why?"

"Because there are so many more white collar workers, more executives, and so few rock bottom, gut jobs that don't exist anymore. Men have been forced to adapt, and have taken the track that if phony and plastic works in their business, it ought to work in their social life too. We women get the fallout from men deliberately being heartless, unfeeling, or making you believe they don't care. That's not human nature, and it's not right. I mean, if you're going to cry behind closed doors and hurt all by yourself, then you're lacking. If you really care about someone and really love them, you shouldn't be ashamed to hurt in front of them.

"At the same time, people you choose to hurt in front of must be receptive and caring about your hurt. They should encourage and invite you to lean on them for temporary support and let you take warmth and comfort from another's strong arms. I stress the word temporary. You might not fix the problem at that moment, but at least it could make it better for a little while ... to allow a breathing spell that may be all you need to solve the problem from your own resources after you're more composed. It annoys me that men are becoming phony and plastic, and too coldhearted."

* * * * * *

I found the women I interviewed to be upbeat, confident, and intelligent. That caused me to wonder about and subsequently ask:

Do you envy any qualities or traits you think are common to males in general?

MORE THAN ANY OTHER TRAIT, more women, seventeen percent of the total, said they envy men's confidence. Within the definition of confidence they included men's take charge ability.

A typical comment was, "There was a time when I envied the ease with which men seemed to do about whatever they wanted. I had to realize on my own that no one had given or denied me permission to be the same way. So now I pack that trait and no longer envy men for it."

A thirty-two-year-old housewife said, "I had a male friend who was completely self-sufficient in everything he did. At the time I admired him, partly because I felt like I was just foundering. But I learned a lot from him about taking control of my life. I think mothers teach sons that trait, and I envy it. But self-sufficiency can be learned by females on their own. I think mothers need to teach that when they're raising a daughter, as equally as they do to sons."

Here is the view of a twenty-four-year-old television news reporter: "I envy the fact that young males are programmed early in life to know what they want and then go for it. Generally, females are programmed to be more passive ... 'Don't make a game plan for your life, because you'll just marry and have children.' I envy males in that they seem to take charge of their lives."

A forty-four-year-old-ad agency owner put her envy of male self-confidence this way: "I don't know if it's inherited or taught, but little boys seem to have a dominant self-confidence that girls have to learn. I was an only child and my parents instilled in me the attitude that I could do anything I wanted. And I have. As far as I'm concerned, self-confidence is learned."

The secretary said, "I envy men not being afraid of going out at night to walk alone. They seem never to be afraid of the dark. As a female I have a lot of fears that a man doesn't. I envy men's assertiveness and society's acceptance of it. I envy that they can change a light bulb without climbing up a ladder."

A quality control clerk for a cellular phone company said, "Males have been taught to take the bull by the horns and be in charge of what happens in their lives. I believe more women are picking up on that and not being victims as much as they used to be. I admire the fact that so many men take action to see that they control their lives."

The second trait the women envied most in males was a man's physical and mental strength. A twenty-seven-year-old convenience store clerk said, "I envy their physical strength. I also envy their mental strength in handling a tough situation on the spot ... a situation where I would have to cry first."

A thirty-three-year-old line service secretary for an airport fixed base operator also envied men's physical strength. "I think women would be considered more equal if we had men's muscle power."

Miscellaneous comments about what women envied in men were:

"Men rise above the little problems that women dwell upon. Men either solve the problem or dismiss it as too small to worry about."

"Most men don't gossip, and I like that."

"I don't envy a man. There's nothing about a man that I envy."

"I envy that a man can go without his shirt and get by with it."

"I envy men's mechanical skills. I'd like to be able to fix the car and the commode and all those things as easily as they do."

"I envy that men don't seem to worry. If I have a problem hanging over me, I don't function well. Some men seem to be able to just put a worry out of their head until they are ready to handle it at their convenience. I wish I could do that."

"I envy a man's ability to slough off a bad day, or blow off something that is said to them, good or bad."

"I think men working together aren't as 'gripey' as women working together. Wish we were like that."

"I think men are taken more seriously than women. For instance, when a woman goes to a bank for a loan, too often the banks say, 'Honey, come back later when your husband has time to come in with you.' I hate that."

"I envy male esprit de corps. They can get together, even if they're married, and have a good ol' time. Lately I've been allowed to join a group of men when they take beer and food down to the river. I am the only female. When I see how they interact, I envy it so much. I feel privileged to join them, and I know the rules ... don't bring up feelings ... they don't want to get thoughtful. Lots of horsing around ... splashing through the water ... rolling in the sand and mud, like a bunch of monkeys. They are so much more physical than women. It's shallow in a way, but I wish women could have silly physical fun that way. Men bond, where women often work against each other."

"I admire the camaraderie that men have with other men. I wish I could experience that. Also, it seems men have a better grip on their emotions, a more constant personality, where women's hormonal fluctuations make them crazy. When I'm crying and I know there is absolutely no reason except that part of my body is making me emotional, I get envious that men can be so level and constant."

One last area where women envy men. A thirty-seven-year-old personnel manager said, "I like their ability to learn from each other, like through a mentor. Women don't seem to have plugged into that yet. Having, or being, a mentor is a wise strategy. I think men's networking is wonderful. Their business abilities are marvelous. There are lots of things I admire about men."

* * * * * *

Most men have occasionally experienced impatience from a woman. To discover if there might be something we could do to dampen or reduce that event, I asked:

What is your opinion as to a weakness you consider common to males in general?

THE MAJORITY (thirty-four percent) said that men often act too macho, and/or posture like peacocks to protect their egos. Twenty-eight percent felt a common weakness in males is their inability to show emotional feelings. An attractive, atomic lab mathematician said, "Some men are so egotistical they can't think with anything but their penis."

The blonde television news anchor laughed at the question and answered, "Their most common weakness is what's in their pants. Beyond that, when another female walks by, I note little loyalty to me. I find men don't have a lot of loyalty to the area covered by my panties, and that aggravates. Gentlemen, here's a little secret: women are never quite satisfied with who they are. We have insecurities. Most of us try to cover those insecurities with makeup, clothes, and constant attention to our figure. I feel insecure when I'm with a man whose eyes fall out when he sees a good looker. Enough is enough. Damn it, either don't pour salt onto my insecurities, or find yourself another woman."

A striking thirty-seven-year-old with a degree in business

administration said: "Most men's egos are in their J-E-A-N-S." She laughed. "My first husband said the reason women don't have brains is because God didn't give them a penis to put them in."

She laughed again and added, "That husband is history. My second husband doesn't feel that way. His brains are in the right place, and so is his ego. I'm keeping him."

A thirty-seven-year-old pawn shop keeper said the weakness she disliked was the need for some men to act macho ... the open shirt with chains around his neck ... the "Me, Tarzan, I am King" syndrome. "At the other end of these macho types, I have a male friend who is six inches shorter than me. I have the utmost respect for him because he has no trace of that macho bit, yet he is one of the strongest males I know."

I asked, "Strong in what way?"

"Sure of himself. Not cocky, but sure of himself, with good reason. He's good at so many things. He's not false, a fine, incredible person."

Regarding the second most repeated (at twenty-eight percent) opinion about male weakness was "not showing true feelings ... inability to cry ... holding in their emotions."

A forty-three-year-old office manager said, "A possible weakness, a weakness more taught to young boys rather than one that's in their genes, is a lack of willingness to express their feelings. For example, I have a friend who had a fishing buddy he spent weekends with in a small, open boat. One weekend when they were fishing, his friend said casually, 'By the way, I got divorced last week.' My friend had no idea anything was awry between the man and his wife. Men have been taught to suppress feelings ... 'Don't cry because that's unmanly.' But since that's socially implanted, men can overcome that. The strong ones, at least."

"The greatest weakness I see," said a twenty-four-year-old airline stewardess, "is their inability to show emotion ... to cry, as if they're afraid someone may judge them as a weeny. I don't see crying as a weakness. To me, it's a strong man who isn't afraid to cry ... let it out and tell me all about it."

Miscellaneous answers as to what women consider a male weakness were: "They tend to play around. They think it's okay as long as you don't know. They are too loose with commitment."

"I think a common male weakness is that men don't trust one another with their emotional stuff as easily as women do. That is a weakness, because it forces men into needing a woman in an intense way for emotional support. If men had each other to share emotional traumas ... to talk out some of their garbage ... there wouldn't be that urgency to be with a woman. I think that would make it easier for men."

"A male weakness? Men don't handle rejection, divorce, or any conflict with a female. It has to do with the way men are raised. As boys, they rarely had to cope with a lot of things, because mothers have a tendency to shelter little sons. Therefore, boys aren't given a chance to be disappointed all that much when they are little. Girls, on the other hand, are taught to stifle their desires ... they are taught they can't do this or that, so girls learn to take disappointment early, and throughout a woman's life, she handles it better. Example: During divorce proceedings, often the stress causes men to falter on the job. A woman, however, tends to buckle down during divorce stress. Her job becomes vital, so she tends to miss less work under stress than a man. Because as youngsters, girls learn early to bend, where too often men aren't forced to learn that skill early in life."

A twenty-eight-year-old manicurist believes, "Men seem insecure about what they think a woman wants in her man, physically or money-wise. Men fear they can't live up to her hopes, so they overcompensate. Many men don't realize the importance a woman places on intelligence. His brains are right at the top of my list."

The young widow of a night freighter pilot killed in a crash said about male weakness, "I think all males are more breakable than females."

"Breakable?" I inquired.

"Emotionally. They are breakable because this big macho masculine figure is expected never to give in to a weakness, such as admitting maybe he's wrong, or crying inside but not showing a thing outside. All these responsibilities we dump on them, and then give them no room for error, or, God forbid, failure.

"I also believe men's sexual performance is very fragile. It must be scary for them to realize they just can't goof, that they must meet social pressures to prove they are all man, all of the time. Sometimes I think men endure so much pressure, they can't be human. Yet, there's a frailty there, like Samson, or Achilles. Those two big strong men each had a tiny weakness that could destroy them.

"Physically, men are obviously stronger than women, but they have a fragile breaking point. Men can be destroyed so easily. I don't see men as wimps, but they are more breakable than we give them credit for. They have a breaking point they don't want anyone else to know exists. I wouldn't want the pressure that is on them to continually pick up the pieces and keep the act together."

After hearing women answer that question, I have an appreciation of their tendency for softness toward what they consider men's weaknesses.

* * * * * *

In my school days, I noticed that girl classmates invariably had a close friendship with one or more females. These female/female friendships seemed tighter than male/male or male/female friendships. In hopes that we males might better understand why women often choose females for best friends, I asked my panel of women,

Is your closest friend male or female, and why?

SIXTY-THREE PERCENT of the women said that a female was their best friend. Reasons they gave were:

"Because she understands my feelings better than a man does. She has the same things on her mind that I do."

"A female is my best friend because I can share anything with her. We can talk about a guy's penis, or anything. With a male, I have to be more careful and not say certain things or discuss certain subjects. I'm on guard with a male, where I'm not with a female."

A school teacher said, "I can be friends with men, but I'm not comfortable because I fear that eventually there may be an attraction. That doesn't happen with a woman friend. It's also easier to talk with a woman about female body problems, and so on."

Another woman said, "My best friend is female, however if I want a straight answer, I'll go to a male."

"Throughout my life a female has been my best friend, but in law school, it was a male."

"There are lots of reasons why a female is my best friend. For one, men are harder to make friends with, because men often translate friendliness into sexual overtones that may not be there. Also, being friendly with a male often makes his woman jealous. And, women tend to remain friends after they marry, but when a man friend gets married, the friendship ends. So, it's not only easier to have a woman friend, it's also more convenient."

A woman who has a male as her best friend said, "I find females narrower and a little catty. When I find a man who is willing to talk to me, I relate more than I do with a woman. I get his point of view on issues, and he gets mine. As a female television reporter, a male view is more valuable to me than a female's."

* * * * * *

In my coming-of-age years, I sensed that most of my male friends seemed to harbor a deep-seated fear of women. Among other things, we were scared to death to ask for dates, especially if an intended was among the prettiest in school. So, I asked the women,

Do you think some men fear women? If so, what do you think they fear?

ONE HUNDRED PERCENT of the women I asked said, yes, they felt some men feared women. Here is a selection of their responses:

A forty-five-year-old teacher believed, "Some men still think that unless a woman is financially dependent upon them, they don't have a foundation to hold her in a relationship. These men fear that today's women don't really need them all that much."

A forty-two-year-old sales manager for a television station said, "Men fear our seeing or knowing of a failure in some area, such as sex. They fear that a woman will get to know them too well. They fear she might decide they were not what she wanted or needed and reject them. They fear overplaying their hand, and revealing themselves for what they are deep down. Maybe that's why men don't talk openly with wives or girlfriends."

The forty-four-year-old radio salesperson believed men fear women because, "They are afraid they might offend their woman, like not doing the 'right' thing. I feel men want to please a woman, but some just don't know how to go about it."

I then asked, "In what areas do you think men worry about pleasing women?"

"A guy doesn't know if I want him to open a door for me, or if I'm going to think he's a male chauvinist for trying to. He doesn't know if he should light my cigarette, or if I'm going to cut him off with, 'Thanks, but I have my own lighter.' He's afraid that if he offers to pay for a weekend, I might say thank you, I can pay my own way."

"Please give the men advice."

"They need to follow their instincts. It's not going to work for them to modify their behavior to satisfy me. In time, we're going to uncover each other anyway, so we might as well get started in the beginning. My advice is, just stumble ahead and damn the torpedoes."

A twenty-nine-year-old secretary said, "I think men fear women trying to swallow them up ... drain them emotionally, financially, and every other way. I believe that's why so many younger people are unmarried. I think men are worried that a woman is going to engulf them."

A twenty-nine-year-old paralegal said, "Men start out being afraid of asking a woman for a date. After they're dating, they are afraid to risk getting too close to the woman. Next, the man fears being dropped. My husband says men fear super-good-looking women ... fear of not standing a chance with her. And if they win her attention, then they fear losing her to some other guy. When I was in school, the prettiest girls weren't asked for dates as often as the more common girls. It took me a while to figure out that an especially attractive female intensifies a man's insecurities. Yeah, men have lots of fears about women."

A twenty-eight-year-old nail salon employee said, "I think men are scared of intimacy."

"Intimacy as in a woman's definition?" I asked. (See page 59)

"Yes."

A twenty-year-old cosmetologist said, "I think a majority of men fear women. They seem to think women want money and cars and things."

"What do you really want?"

"Love, respect, trust."

A forty-six-year-old counselor said, "Both men and women have a magical thing about our mothers, and how she brought us into the world. But at about three or four, little girls figure out that they are built just like mother. It's then that being female is no big deal to a girl, and girls become less impressed about motherhood being magical. But to men, females always seem to be another species. Who are they, and why do they act like such and such? We're scary to men ... maybe it's our hormones. Whatever, men fear just about everything about a woman."

The motel night clerk said, "Sure, men fear women, and they should."

"Why?"

"Because we're mean and sneaky. Not up front about a lot of things. We go around and get you in the back. I would much rather work with a group of men ... hell, I fear some women too."

A forty-three-year-old counselor said, "Men fear women's expectations, fear they may not be able to live up to the demands of some women. Like being everything to her and taking care of her in every way ... emotionally, financially, and sexually. Most men aren't up to all of that, they know it, and it scares them."

A thirty-seven-year-old lawyer said, "Men I know are afraid a woman might be superior to them, either in making more money, or the fact that a woman is learning more. Men seem to hit a spot in life where they are content, and just stop. Most women I know continue to go to school, try to learn, and achieve. I think men fear women like that."

A twenty-eight-year-old hair stylist said, "Men are afraid that a woman is going to get her claws into them and restrict them. I think they fear being tied down. I think they fear being responsible for taking care of her children and not having a chance to live their own lives, to do whatever they want."

A thirty-seven-year-old housewife who described herself as a "Domestic Goddess" said, "Men fear us because they don't understand us. They see us as an enigma, and I think that's great, because as long as they're wondering, they're interested. With all this chemistry going on in a woman's body, creating all these moods, changes the bait pretty often. As long as our hormones make us different from day to day, we'll remain mysterious and never boring. Men are afraid of our unknowns. Thank God. Otherwise, they might turn to watching sunsets ... heaven forbid."

A forty-eight-year-old bank executive secretary said, "I think men fear women's sensitivity to situations and other people. Some people call it woman's intuition, but that's a misnomer. It's a sensitivity women get at birth. For example, a woman can walk into a room where there are people and tell if someone has just had an argument, whether someone has just told a joke, whether someone has just finished making love, or whether someone has just had a deep, 'clear the air' kind of conversation. Men can walk into that same room and not sense any of those things. Men are oblivious, living in a world of their own. I think men fear women's sensitivity because they don't understand it. They put our 'intuition' in the category of voodoo and black magic. That's why a lot of men consider women mysterious."

Here are shorter answers that some women gave:

"I think they fear the unknown about us. They don't know what to expect, or what to do, and that scares 'em."

An airline pilot said, "I think men are intimidated by my flying ability."

"Women are moody. Men fear not knowing if they're doing the right thing. They fear the unknown in women."

"Men fear that they won't deliver what they think a woman expects, that they won't measure up as far as being good looking enough, tall enough, have a good job, etc. They are afraid we might be too judgmental."

"I think men fear strong women. A weak man especially fears a strong woman. Also, they fear a woman who has the potential to make more money or have a better job."

"Men fear entrapment."

The ad agency owner said, "They're scared to death of us. Afraid we're going to 'take them,' or be smarter than them, or that their role as the dominant force may take a back seat. They fear that we may discover they are weak."

I wanted to know, "How do you define a strong man?"

"One who is not fearful of women and who knows his own mind and follows it."

A fifty-six-year-old housewife and family business bookkeeper said, "Today, men are afraid of women because we have so many options. When women were in the caves, the women had two choices about their lives: like it, or lump it. And as little as fifty years ago, society said of unhappy women, 'You made your bed, and by God you can lie in it.' Men fear women because we don't have to take it anymore ... we can bug out anytime we get fed up." She smiled. "Treat a woman with respect, guys, and you'll have no reason to fear her."

* * * * * *

As a follow-up, I asked:

How do you think many men perceive women?

THE BANK EXECUTIVE SECRETARY said, "i don't think they perceive us. They look at us, they wonder about us, they want to know about us, they need us, they love us, but they don't understand us."

A fifty-year-old housewife believes, "Men think a woman is looking for a meal ticket. They also see a woman as just one more notch on their penis.

"Example: a guy was putting the make on me. He said, 'Well, I'm checked for AIDS every six months.' To go with this guy would be like using the public bathroom down at the courthouse or at the airport. He was a piece of public property. How sad that he would think that all I was interested in was that he is checked for AIDS. Obviously he not only doesn't think much of 'wimmin,' he doesn't think much of himself either."

One of the counselors said, "Men see women as puzzling. At the same time they seem to be enchanted with women and feel like they can't live without us. Most men get their emotional needs filled by women ... sweethearts, wives, mothers, daughters, sisters, etc."

A thirty-one-year-old lawyer believes, "Men see us as a burden. Clinging and manipulative. They also see us as sex objects, to be used a while and then treated as if we were a pain in the butt to have around."

The probation officer said, "Too many men underestimate a woman's abilities and can't appreciate her as a person. Men's perceptions of women aren't focused. We understand more about men than they understand about us."

Another lawyer said, "Men think we're all easy lays. They also think we're after their money, and that we want to change them. I'm a changer. I know it causes trouble, but I try anyway. If I found a guy I really liked, if he didn't have something that needed fixing, I'd probably let him go. I'd be unhappy if there wasn't something about him I could fix."

A thirty-eight-year-old department store salesperson said, "A lot of men today are out for what they can get out of women. They just use them ... maybe because they've had one bad experience. From that, they lump all women into one category and just use them. They're being unfair to themselves, and to women."

A forty-three-year-old retail salesperson said, "Most men view us as an enigma, mysterious, sneaky, and devious." She laughed. "I find that hilarious ... comical ... hysterical. I love it."

A thirty-nine-year-old housewife said, "With women's lib, there's a war between a lot of men and women. That's sad. I like our differences. It's neat that a woman can flirt, and that men can flirt back. I think men should see women not as dumb broads. I'm not after his job. I enjoy being a woman and all that goes with it, and I enjoy a man and all that he is. But it seems a lot of men resent women, to the point of vengeance, and that's scary. We may talk big, but in the face of a mean, raving man, we are helpless. Men, from their hormones or whatever, can be very frightening physically to a woman. When a woman sleeps with a man, she is giving him everything she has, including complete trust. Yet, that man is big enough to beat her senseless. News stories remind us that we can't be too careful about which men to trust. That scares us."

A forty-five-year-old teacher said, "Men see women as necessary to their lives. They need a woman more than a woman needs a man. That scares 'em. Maybe that need comes from their having come into the world via a woman, and then having their lives depend upon a woman for some years. I spent eight years on my own, and wasn't threatened by it. I'm my husband's third wife, and he was never single more than a couple of months. I think men perceive women as loving, giving, and selfless. It confuses them when they discover that many women are selfish. I think they see us only clearly in what they think we can do for them."

A forty-two-year-old woman's dress shop owner said, "Men perceive women as a necessary item in their lives. I think a man needs a woman. I don't think a woman needs a man. Men see women as a complement to him ... an accessory ... like a tape deck in his vehicle."

A twenty-seven-year-old clerical worker in an office said, "I think the average Joe thinks women like to shop and spend money. Most men don't realize how intelligent women are. They see us as the weaker sex and don't look much for brains."

Other comments as to how women think men perceive them were: "To most men, I think we're sex objects."

"Too often men perceive us as not being intelligent."

"They see us first as sex objects, then as second mothers."

"They see us as someone to mother their children, keep house, and be a sex partner."

"Weak and passive, or as bitches."

"Men see us as dipsy. They don't expect a lot out of us."

"They don't see us as equals. Most men want an intelligent woman, but she'd better not be smarter than he is ... not even once."

"They see us as silly, uninformed, and unable to handle responsibility."

"Men see women as dependent."

"As dumb ... inferior."

"As part of a pursuit game. To conquer. As objects to be won. A trophy."

"As a pleasure toy."

"A lot of men see women as basic airheads. They also think we're stupid, dingy, and poor drivers."

A thirty-three-year-old professional pilot for an air charter service said, "Younger men see us as things. They view us as fun for a little while ... entertainment for them. On the other hand, older men see women as more special. They see us as people they want to get to know ... they see us as interesting. My man is an older man."

When I showed this work to some of the women I had interviewed, they asked me to emphasize that not all men see women in a negative way. They pointed out that there are some gallant, respectful gentlemen out there who genuinely respect women. Their complaint was that these men seem few and far between.

*   *   *   *   *   *

After reviewing the above comments, I wondered how women felt about men as friends. I asked,

On a scale of zero to ten, how important is it that you have an ongoing close friendship with a man?

THE AVERAGE IMPORTANCE the women put on a close friendship with a male was 8.6. Values ranged from a couple of zeros to a couple of twenties. Comments about having a close friendship with a man were:

"Definitely a ten. Without friendship first, you don't have anything, because friendship leads to everything else."

"Nine. I enjoy being around men. I like working where men work."

A marriage counselor had these observations: "The biggest hassle is being clear and open with each other about the friendship's limits. A healthy friendship with a male is one that makes it clear that anything they do, each can tell or show to their partner. That's a healthy monitor. It's what to say to a potential male friend. Point out that if he can stay within that boundary, and feel okay about it, then he has a friend in you. But, if you're involved in conversations or actions you wouldn't want repeated to your spouse, then you're into something other than a friendship. Women need men as friends, but without all that sexual stuff.

"The sexual stuff can be a hassle because the pull of sex is so strong. Face it, we are the sexiest creatures on earth. We can't run as fast as a deer; our eyes aren't as sharp as an eagle's; our ears aren't as sensitive as most animals; we don't have fur, or natural clothes; and so on. As a species, what has made us successful is that we mate all of the time. We don't have to wait for a season, and we do sex for a lot of reasons other than to reproduce. For those of us who walk the earth today, the cost is that we are the result of the sexiest of the sexiest. Because we are highly sexual, it's almost impossible for humans to have any kind of male/female relationship without sex hovering in the shadows. That's probably why women place a high value on having an ongoing close friendship with a male. For me it's a seven."

The thirty-six-year-old electronic repair technician said, "Twenty for me. If I have a spat with my significant other, I want a male friend to talk to and get his point of view, because men are weird. They think so much differently than women, I sometimes need their weird opinions."

A fifty-year-old widow said, "I wish I had a man friend like my best female friend. Then I could get a man's honest view without having to hang on to my panties. I'd give my left arm for a male friend I could talk to openly, one I could feel as safe with as I do my best female friend. A male I could call and ask to be taken to a party without him reading into the invitation that he can get into my pants in exchange. I'd give a lot for a male friend like that."

Allow me to give one male's viewpoint on how a woman might best develop a male friendship without sexual implications. Some men are also anxious to eliminate the boy-girl thing and serve only as a dancing partner, movie escort, or party companion. However, male egos being what they are, the woman should be first to propose this arrangement. The woman should take the lead, because a male is afraid to propose a nonsexual relationship with a woman for fear that you or your friends might ask, "What's wrong with this guy?"

In other words, he's afraid you or friends may think he's gay. By your taking the lead, you blunt his fear of your thinking such. You may be pleasantly surprised at how receptive, even relieved, some men will be to the idea of a friendship without sexual pressures. You could have your cake and eat it too ... the advantages of a male relationship in a less tense atmosphere. Under that umbrella, you have an opportunity to improve your appraisals of each other, in less time. And who's to say where your discoveries may end, or lead? *A note to men*: To appreciate the importance women might place on a platonic relationship, check their answers to our next question—they were eye openers for me.

* * * * * *

The next question had two parts:

What is your definition of intimacy? What do you believe intimacy means to a man?

I WAS SURPRISED TO LEARN that women have a definition of intimacy far different from a man's. One hundred percent of the women felt intimacy was a mental connection. Ninety-three percent of these same women said they thought a man's definition of intimacy was sex.

For example, our thirty-three-year-old line service secretary at a private airport defined intimacy as, "being so verbally close that you can say anything to him ... absolutely anything ... share your most private thoughts. And of course, he must share what makes him tick, his fears, his dreams. Intimacy is feeling comfortable at being completely open, with no fear of criticism or judgement. Without that feeling, there is no intimacy as far as I'm concerned."

I asked, "What do you think your man's definition of intimacy is?"

"Sex."

Another example: "Intimacy is being able to look right into my little darling's eyes and tell him exactly what I feel and think. And him caring enough to look me right back." She laughed. "His definition? Sex, with a capital S."

The forty-four-year-old radio advertising sales person said: "Intimacy is talking ... being able to talk about anything and everything. That's being close."

"What do you think his definition is?"

"Being in bed, naked as a jay bird."

Other comments:

"A closeness where someone knows everything about you, and you are comfortable enough to be yourself."

"His definition?"

"Sex."

"Intimacy is where the barriers are down, and you can talk on any subject with each other on a deeply personal level. In time, that may lead into sexual overtones, but not in the beginning." She smiled. "My husband's definition of intimacy is sex."

A doctor's wife said, "That question has lots of levels, because there are lots of levels of intimacy. If a woman has lunch with a man, that's one level. They are probably going to talk superficially, not covering anything deep, especially in the daytime. For some reason, when you get into the deeper level of personal feelings and the nitty gritty of the situation, it's almost always in the evening, or wee early hours. I think intimacy has to be worked at constantly. It has to be striven for. It begins with sharing mentally. There may be casual caresses that aren't sexual but by accident or design will build into sexual caresses."

"His definition?"

"A good lay."

A forty-one-year-old diagnostic technician said, "Intimacy is sharing everything together, putting all our cards on the table. When someone says to me they have an intimate relationship, I take that to mean they are as close as two people can be."

"His definition?"

"Wham, bam, thank you, ma'am."

A twenty-seven-year-old waitress said, "His definition of intimacy is sex. His definition is about a five on the scale. But my kind of intimacy has to do with your heart, and how far you're gonna' let me into your head. My kind of intimacy rates a ten plus."

A thirty-five-year-old secretary said, "If a man thinks sex is intimacy, he's talking about fake intimacy, and I feel sorry for him. Apparently he hasn't ever really known the joy of knowing a woman through the give and take of risky, scary, beautiful discovery via mental intercourse with each other. Sex, after a mental trip like that, is literally out of this world."

She sighed. "I'd do anything in bed for a man who is interested enough to really get to know me." She looked me in the eye. "Bed-hopping sex is fake intimacy. If he thinks that is being intimate with a woman, he has the mind of a moron, the penis of a jackass, and the heart of a wimp."

A forty-five-year-old California high school teacher said, "Intimacy is a state of mind between two people. Connecting mentally is the best way you fulfill each other in those special ways. Intimacy is a closeness shared through a mental touching of minds and thoughts. Intimacy creates bonding."

"His definition?"

She laughed. "Sex."

The apparent difference between a woman's and a man's definition of intimacy highlights the difference in how men and women see the world, By the dictionary, "close association" is intimacy, and so is "sex." Technically, both definitions are correct, yet the social applications of "intimacy" are apparently miles apart.

The difference seems to be either social or the difference between male and female brains. Either way, after hearing these women, I better understand why wives and girlfriends tend to get upset when their man "talks" with another woman. Obviously, in their view he is being "intimate" with another.

That strikes my male brain as a bit oppressive, or at least possessive. And for a man to be accused of being intimate under those terms might be irritating, because he takes that to mean he had sex with her. Connie Hacker of Amarillo suggests we may need a new word for intimacy that is acceptable to both male and female brains. "Intoverse" is a word she suggests to describe a close friendship between males and females that doesn't include sex.

From what the women said, it seems safe to say, "The way to a woman's heart is through her head."

I know men who seem genuinely to understand that and who enjoy interacting with women on that basis. However, I've noticed other men who apparently use courtship only as a means to an end and who try to get it over with as quickly as possible. One ploy they seem to use to expedite things is to mouth the words, "I love you." To determine how women react when men say those three little words, I asked:

When a man says he loves you, what does that mean to you?

THE AUTHOR/SPEAKER SAID, "If I don't know him well, I would say he is either on drugs or incredibly insecure and desperate. If I know the person well, it means he is forming a bond with me."

A brunette officer worker said, "It's according to the situation and what I know about the man. I've had men tell me they loved me on a first coke date. It was so flip it totally turned me off. On the other hand, when my husband finally got up the courage, which was after we had gone together quite a while, his telling me he loved me meant a lot. It was enough to win me."

Another office worker chimed in, "I agree. Some guys on the first date have given me that 'I love you, I can't live without you' line. To myself, I said, 'Yeah, fella, you just want to jump in bed.' My husband seldom tells me he loves me, but from the way we interact, he doesn't have to tell me that constantly. That's the difference between genuine and phony."

The housewife who described herself as a Domestic Goddess lit a cigarette and thought a moment. "It can mean several things. It can mean he's feeling a bond between the two of us. At the other end of the scale, it can mean he wants something from me ... go to bed with him ... don't leave ... or whatever. I think sometimes 'I love you' is a gambit. I evaluate the person and the situation before I take it hook, line, and sinker."

One woman said, "When my man says he loves me, I know he cares deeply for me and my feelings. And it covers more than just loving me sexually. He chooses places and times at odd moments to tell me ... not just when we're in bed. Those odd places and times give his declaration more emotional power. It's nice. I get the feeling that he really loves me, in and out of bed."

A twenty-six-year-old single office worker said, "That's vague with me. Men have told me that who weren't around long after they said it. The words don't carry much weight with me. Actions speak more than their words."

A forty-one-year-old accountant said, "Usually when he says it, it is associated with sex. That isn't to say he doesn't feel it in other ways at other times, but during sex is when I hear it most, and I think he means 'Thank you.' It bothers me that sex is about the only time I hear it."

A forty-four-year-old English teacher said, "If you don't know the person well, and it's said in a moment of passion, it means nothing to me. It's like that's when you're required to say it. But, if saying 'I love you' is declared by a long term partner you know well, it means I love you for what you do for me; I love you because you support me; I love you because of your personality, etc." She paused. "A male friend once advised me not to marry someone I loved, because a lot of responsibility comes with love. Love includes not only sex, but a lifestyle, including sometimes doing things for another that you may not particularly want or like to do ... but that's part of the package. So I measure a man's willingness to take the responsibilities that go with loving someone. If he's willing to have bread most of the time and cake once in a while, he has my attention when he says he loves me. Otherwise, it doesn't mean much."

An assistant district attorney said, "When I was twenty-one, it meant 'I want sex with you'. Now I'm thirty-one and better at selecting men. Today it means he loves me in a way that a woman wants to be loved ... to be appreciated for what she is."

The TV news photographer said, "In the past it meant 'I'm going to rip your heart out and eat it for lunch.' In my experience with one man, it was just a way for him to get what he wanted before he moved on. To talk about it now brings me to tears." She wiped her eyes. "Obviously, it's sad for me." She paused. "I pretty much thought I'd worked through that, but I guess there's pain left."

She lit a cigarette, and exhaled. "I've had men tell me they loved me, and I think they did, but it was never said in an ongoing intimate relationship. It was said to me by men friends I trusted and was close to but never intimate with. But when someone that I was intimately involved with said that, my fear button went off. They seemed to think if they said that, they had license to abuse me, not physically but mentally. I wish I could change that. I would like to believe I could have an intimate relationship where someone says I love you, and then show they mean it by acting like it. Better still, act like you love me first, *then* tell me. But love is such a nebulous term ... I mean, what the hell is love?

"There's a song, 'What Is This Thing Called Love?' God, if the songwriters don't know, don't expect John Doe to know either." She smiled and flicked ash from her cigarette. "But we do know that J.D. loves pizza, or Bic lighters. Sometimes that's how disposable love is. "Whoops my Bic is empty. Oh well, into the trash." She drew on her cigarette. "Before I ever hear 'I love you' again, I want friendship first. I prefer him to say, 'I really like you,' because that's real to me. 'Love' gets lost in the Hollywood fantasy of, 'Oh, kind sir ... since you love me, I'm supposed to give you all of my being.' Right after that, Hollywood goes out the window, and I know he's gonna stomp me. I would like for a man to understand what he's saying when he says he loves me."

She drew on her cigarette again. "Sometimes I think I get too intellectual about it because I'm in such fear." She looked me in the eye. "Define love to me, and then I'll tell you whether or not I can accept your 'I love you' statement." She shrugged. "But imagine asking some man to define what love means. For him just to say the word is about all he can handle. And when he does, too often it means 'I want to screw you', or, 'Now that I've said it, will you cook dinner for me ... do my laundry, screw me again.' 'I love you' is just a coin some men spend for something they want."

She shook her head and looked at the floor. "Love has been so abused. Sometimes I think men use it because they hurt inside, and the 'L' word is easier than kicking the dog. Some men think that after they say 'I love you,' they don't have to do anything else. Those three little words are supposed to make everything fine and wonderful and excuse them from really showing they care. Love is a sacred word to me. If someone says 'I love you,' I check for motives. It means more to me when I'm shown rather than told. Actions speak louder than words. If you love me, I'll know that by your behavior."

She snubbed her cigarette, shrugged, and wiped her eyes.

The flying service VP said, "'I love you' is such a broad term. A man can love spaghetti. Or, if he's a pig farmer, he can love pigs. You can love a lot of things, but that doesn't mean you're kindred spirits."

A thirty-eight-year-old housewife said, "'I love you' has different meanings for different men. I think for most, it means you're gonna be his main squeeze in the future. Those who don't know us well think we want to hear it. I get a big kick out of those guys, and I'm saying to myself, 'Oh, if you only knew me darlin' ... ha, ha. You're taking a chance, Big Boy, talking to me like that when you don't know what a bitchy tiger I can be." She laughed. "As far as I'm concerned, the joke's on him."

The forty-two-year-old personnel manager said, "A person who really means it generally doesn't say it to you soon after he meets you. It's an emotion that takes time to cook as he gets to know me. Then, if it's said in a warm, tender way, it has meaning. Then I believe it's coming primarily from his heart. The message I get is that he honestly cares about me and that I'm special to him."

The utility company parts manager said, "Ninety-eight percent of the time it means he wants sex. Other times it tells me he needs someone, and he wants me to be there for him. He wants to be mothered."

The probation officer believes, "'I love you' means he sincerely loves me and is not just mouthing words. I take him seriously."

A thirty-one-year-old lawyer said, "It's usually a prelude to him attempting to lead me toward the bedroom."

A different district attorney's assistant said, "Some guys tell every woman they love them, while for others, it's like pulling teeth to say those three little words."

I asked, "What's your impression of the guy who tells all the women he loves them?"

"He wants sex. He wants to use her, and he says 'I love you' to make it easier." She laughed. "The guy for whom it's like pulling teeth, when he says it, he's *really* hard up."

The bank secretary said, "If it's a guy you're just dating ... say two dates ... he thinks or hopes that will get you into bed. But if it's your husband and you have a solid, loving marriage, that means he likes you, wants you, and is in love with you. Being in love with somebody and loving somebody are two different animals. Men don't understand that. Loving somebody, like loving a friend with no sexual connection, means that you would prevent something bad from happening to them. You wish them only good, but that wouldn't include going to bed. But when you're in love, you want to do everything with that person ... go to bed with him, fix his meals, wash his clothes, etc. You want to give to him. Giving may be the key word. I am a giving person to someone I'm in love with. Otherwise, I'm only courteous and polite."

The forty-three-year-old president of a personnel pool said, "If it's a man with whom I've had a relationship for over six months, I think he's saying he cares about me and likes my company, and 'It's just me and you, babe.' But if I've barely met the man, he isn't in love, he's in lust. He's using 'I love you' as a shortcut to my bed. How arrogant! He can't love me, because he hasn't had a chance to know me. I chuckle at his stupidity."

The twenty-nine-year-old secretary said, "It depends on how old the relationship is when they say it. Early on, it means we need to slow down, and back off, because that's a bit soon to expect us to know each other on that level. If it's a developed relationship, for him to say he loves me means the world to me. It would mean this man is mine, that he's going to let me continue to share his life emotionally, as a companion and sexually ... the whole bit. It means he's willing to give one hundred percent. For him to tell me he loves me at that stage means so much."

The radio advertising salesperson laughed and said, "When a man tells me he loves me, it means he has extraordinarily good taste in women." She smiled. "And I take him to mean it."

The twenty-nine-year-old paralegal said, "I love you says he is considering a long term relationship with me, and that we won't see anybody else until he has his chance."

A forty-four-year-old bank purchasing agent said, "Before my present husband, it meant nothing to me. It was just a line to get sex. The only time I heard it was in or near the bedroom. After he had shot his wad, it was 'Good night, Irene.' With my present husband, he tells me he loves me when I'm washing dishes, or when I'm all dolled up, or when I'm dusting. His saying it tells me I'm important to him. It gives me a good feeling."

The doctor's wife said, "If a man's actions tell you he loves you, it doesn't matter if he tells you once a day or once a week. His actions say 'I love you' much louder than words."

Some random comments were:

"I think it means that I'll do for a while. I take it with a grain of salt."

"It means that I've connected to his emotions. When he says he loves me, it means I'm important to him and he doesn't want to lose me."

"When he says he loves me, I believe he's saying he will be loyal to me."

A thirty-two-year-old secretary said, "I think a man's 'I love you' has totally different meaning than a woman's. When a guy says it, I think it is for the moment ... that instant, probably in hopes that sex will follow. It's shallow with men. But when a woman says I love you, they have thought about it a lot, and it has deeper meaning. For a woman, it's forever. With men, it doesn't necessarily mean it will be good through tomorrow ... or in fact through more than one round of sex."

The motel night clerk had a lot to say about what "I love you" means to her. "If it's not phony, I take it to mean 'I care about you, I respect you, I try to understand you ... you're important to me ... you're warm ... kind ... loving, and generous.'"

I asked, "How do you separate what might be a phony from a genuine 'I love you' ... what do you watch for?"

"Talk is cheap. I want to see that he loves me. I didn't fall off the first turn of the wagon that rolled into town. When a guy first tells me he loves me, I say to myself, 'That's nice.' But as our time progresses, if he becomes uncaring, egotistical, selfish, orders me around like a slave, stays late at bars, spends his money stupidly and then wants a part of mine too, or just spends his money at the bar and says, 'Oh well, that's the way it is, babe,' ... those things say his 'I love you' was bullshit.

"On the other hand, if time shows he cares and shares, and is sensitive to my needs and desires, then I move toward believing him. I have a basic philosophy about a man: 'Don't walk in front of me, because I might not follow; don't walk behind me, because I don't always know where I'm going either; just walk beside me and hold my hand and be my friend.' He's got to like me, and be my friend before he can be my lover. For him to tell me or tell other people that he likes me says that he respects me and is interested in me. It says he tries to understand me and will be there through thick or thin. Being a friend and liking me is more important than the three little words. It's well and good to say you love somebody ... that's easily done in the heat of passion, or because you think that's what you are expected to say. But for a man to honestly say he loves me says that he accepts me, warts and all.

"Liking somebody is harder than loving them. In our society you can get married in six or seven hours and divorced in thirty minutes. Love was the reason for its beginning, and lack of same for its ending. We have friends from years past that we really liked, really cared about, even from grade school that we still like and care about. How many of us are still in love with the person we thought we loved back in our grade school days? It's so easy to *fall* crazy in love, but it's hard to *stay* there. When love begins to melt, you sure as hell better like that person. To fall crazy in love hardly takes any effort, but liking and being a best friend takes work. Liking is more all-encompassing than love. Liking somebody involves respect, cooperation, understanding, and forgiveness. To like is deeper than to love. Not as passionate, nor crazy, and maybe not as much momentary fun. Certainly less concerned with the way they look ... the shape of their body, or the way they comb their hair. To honestly like a person gets down to the rock bottom of them, including when they are angry, happy, mourning, and so on. A genuine like for someone is usually more lasting and durable. So skip the 'I love you' crap. Just tell me you *like* me, and show it, and I'm all yours, Baby Cakes."

And this from the twenty-four-year-old television reporter: "To be told I'm loved is *almost* the ultimate compliment."

I asked, "What's the ultimate?"

"To be told I'm cherished. To be cherished is above being told I'm loved. I can love a person without being in love with them, but to be cherished is to be valued. That makes me feel special."

* * * * * *

Ever since I became aware of the difference between males and females, I've wondered what makes us attractive to a woman. So I asked them:

What attracts you to a man?

THE SANTA FE SHOP OWNER said, "The most important thing is the way he carries himself. It's almost an athletic quality. They move as if they were comfortable inside their skin. Like if you see a dog that's been beaten, he acts beaten. No zip ... no confidence. Same with a man ... if he's confident, he's comfortable in his skin, like a wild animal is comfortable in its skin. I'm also attracted to a guy who likes what he's doing. And I like men who are alert to what's going on around them."

The twenty-four-year-old television reporter said, "I'm attracted to a man who has a mind and uses it, someone who can think things through and is able to express his thoughts. I don't necessarily mean world politics, but things that are on his mind. I want him to be able to analyze job and social situations ... to be able to figure things out. To me that's more attractive than physical looks. I don't like it if they are built like a body builder. I have no use for muscles. If that's all he has, I prefer not knowing him."

The night manager of a convenience store said, "Eyes are what I see first, and then his rear end. I know his rear is a good one when I want to pat it."

The retail salesperson said, "I'm attracted to a man who talks to me, first, and listens to me, second. That's more important to me than so-called handsome."

A thirty-seven-year-old housewife said, "I love a man who has a brilliant mind and command of the English language. It doesn't matter what he looks like. My attorney has a face like a fish and a shape like a frog. But I'm helplessly attracted to him because he's so smart. It's much more fun to be around a man who stimulates your mind. I could listen to him talk all night. But to sit for hours with some handsome, dumb dude? I get tired of saying, 'Wow, isn't he handsome.' That's gets old fast. But if he stimulates my head, there will always be something new. With a guy like that, life can never get dull."

The forty-four-year-old ad agency owner is attracted to "his brightness. Someone who can talk to me … someone who can think and isn't afraid to ask how I feel about things. Between marriages I went with a lot of guys. When I came home, I knew everything about them: how much child support they paid, where they lived, where they went to school, what their interests were, etc. At the end of our date, the only thing they knew about me was where to pick me up."

The twenty-nine-year-old secretary said, "I'm turned on by his intelligence. It's also important that he be able to communicate. For him to carry on an intelligent conversation with me is a real turn on. Musicians attract me because they seem good at communicating. Additionally, they communicate through music."

The bank secretary said, "I have to see his eyes. From his eyes I get a clue to his honesty, and a clue to how he sizes me up. Does he like what he sees? One time a guy got my eye, and he kept waiting for me to look away. I wouldn't. He came over and said, 'You dared me, didn't you?' I admitted I did. At the time, I was bitter and mad at men, so I dared him with a look that said, 'If you think you're man enough to handle me, here l am.' I didn't play the sweet demure thing … I challenged. My look also said, 'Okay, let's see if you can deliver what you're promising.' He asked me to coffee. I could tell from his eyes, as well as what he said, that he was attracted to me."

The thirty-three-year-old airline transport pilot said, "I'm attracted to a good vocabulary. Also, I pick up on how he feels about himself. I can sense that, especially with older men. Young boys, which they are until they are thirty, don't even know why they are on this earth. I also pick up on the way they stand, walk, talk, dress, the things they do, and the kind of friends they have. When I worked line service, I looked at their hands when they signed their gas ticket. When I saw a handsome hand, usually a handsome face went with it. I also noticed if they were left or right handed. Neat fingernails told me they were neat and cared about themselves."

A sixteen-year-old high school student said, "I look at how they present themselves in a crowd. Some guys put on a big macho show and never bring out who they really are. They just put up a front. If they can't show who they are, maybe they're ashamed of it. I'm attracted to a guy who isn't afraid to show who he really is."

A forty-one-year-old cattle ranch owner said, "I'm attracted by his character first, and second by how they handle whatever they do. It doesn't matter so much what he does, so long as he does it to the best of his ability. As for character, I don't like shady movies, foul language, or girlie magazines. Those habits are flashing neon signs saying that this is a shallow, narrow person. I'd have trouble listening to him because of where he was coming from."

The thirty-nine-year-old television news photographer said, "Sometimes I'm hit with basic animal scent, and boy has that gotten me bad choice after bad choice. Now I force myself to pay attention to men who think. I find them a nice change from the football mentality ... 'Futball 'as ben berry berry gud ta me.' I'm interested in, 'Can you speak to me?. . hello? . . can we talk about the idea of growth?. . your plans for the future?' A man who faces questions like that is what I'm looking for. 'Gimmie a beer.' Give me a break. 'Ey, move ... move ... I'm try'n 'a watch th' game, okay.' 'Yes dear. You want a sandwich, dear?'" She laughed. "After wasting my time on a couple of those, I'll never go for one again."

A lawyer said, "I used to go by physical appearance, but that's not important anymore. The older I get, the more his personality attracts me. I can get past a lot of physical if his personality is good."

The camera repair person said, "When I was a clinging vine, there wasn't a good relationship in my life. Now that my self-confidence is high, I do okay. I'm attracted to intelligent self-confident men."

The Associated Press photographer said, "I'm attracted to a combination of intelligence, wit, and physical features. I can be friends with men who have only one or two of those, but for me to be involved, I need all three in one man."

A chamber of commerce secretary said, "I want common interests. At the same time, if a guy drives up in a Rolls Royce, he's going to get my attention real quick. And when he gets out, if he's neat and clean, then hey, I'm ready to strike up a conversation. We're going to find some common interests, old buddy."

The twenty-six-year-old cardiovascular technician said, "I'm turned on by intelligence and wit. Also, I like to watch a man tackle a challenging situation and observe how he handles himself. If he passes that test, I'm a pushover."

*   *   *   *   *   *

Most men have probably wondered what makes us sexy to a woman? For clues I requested them to:

Describe your version of a sexy man.

BEFORE BEGINNING THE PROCESS of selecting their best answers for use in this section, I sensed the question may have been redundant to previous questions. However, reviewing their answers taught me that women have definitions that are more finely tuned than most males'. Note the differences between their answers to the previous question, *What attracts you to a man*, and their version of a sexy man.

The CPA secretary said, "Sexiness comes in the way he looks at me, more than what I see in him physically. The way he looks at me ... not the way I look at him."

"How does he look at you that makes him sexy?" I asked.

"When I see that it makes him feel good to look at me. If we're talking, it's a look that says he would like to step nearer, that he would like to enter my space ... a look that says he wants to know me better. To me that is sex, and it is wonderful sex."

The forty-four-year-old bank purchasing agent said, "Sexy to me is courteous, attentive, and honestly interested in who I am. Sexiness is not physical with me. The younger ones don't understand that."

A forty-three-year-old counselor said, "Sexiness doesn't depend on being handsome in the traditional sense. Sexiness is based more on the appeal of his personal characteristics. Good grooming is also important. So is a sense of humor, intelligence, a sense of perspective. To me, a man who scares small children and animals is not sexy."

The twenty-eight-year-old nail salon employee said a sexy man "has really gorgeous eyes, eyes that see right through me. A man who is confident, and sometimes kind of a bad boy type. I find 'bad boy' sexy, one who looks like he would be trouble to get involved with. I think those kinds of guys are really sexy."

One of the counselors said, "A sexy man has good eye contact, a sense of humor, and a sense of enjoying being in his own body, a body he moves well with, that food tastes good to, and that is affected by music. Also, tactile things are neat to him ... he responds to the feel of fabrics, such as clothing. And he's comfortable with his own sexuality so that he doesn't have to show off how sexy he is. He has a self-assuredness about him."

A retail salesperson said, "Physical may be the first bait, but it's not what catches me. He's got to have substance to hook me."

Another woman's opinion was, "A man is sexy to me who appreciates the things I do for him and lets me know about it. Sexiness for me is more the emotional outlook than physical. It's how he allows me to feel about not only myself, but how I feel about myself when I'm with him. Also, it's how we feel about our relationship. There's nothing sexier than a good relationship between us."

The forty-four-year-old ad agency owner said, "A sexy man is one who knows how to make me feel good. It's not how he looks, it's how he acts ... the way he touches the back of my neck, or the way he holds me when we dance, or the way he talks to me on the phone. Physical appearance may be an early attraction, but if the rest is not there, I'm gone."

The motel night clerk said that for her, sexy was, "A man who is clean, warm, gentle, kind, quick to laugh, not ashamed to cry, and aware of what is going on in my day. I believe eyes are windows to our soul. A mouth can lie, but eyes are honest. The man doesn't have to fit within a certain age or stature or body frame. Sexiness has more to do with the size of his heart, the breadth of his mind, and how much room he has for me."

A fifty-two-year-old teacher from Alabama said, "Sexy to me is a man who feels good about himself, a man who is confident, who doesn't ask my opinion every time he launches a project or chooses clothes. Sexy is a man who isn't insecure. Intelligence is also sexy. A mind that plays and can jump around turns me on so much it is incredible. I also find it sexy when a man is physically active, and who can fall on his face and get up grinning. I fell in love with a guy because when he went skating for the first time in his life, he could fall and get right up and try again, without being destroyed. One more thing that is absolutely the sexiest. In pictures of men in those magazines, they aren't sexy at all until I come to a picture of a guy looking me right in the eye. Good eye contact is absolutely the sexiest thing that can happen."

The fifty-six-year-old housewife and family business bookkeeper said, "Appearance isn't that much. He could be the cutest male ever put on earth, but if he doesn't have two brain cells rubbing together, forget sex."

For one woman, "Sexy is a man who has a mind powerful enough to seduce me with."

Another said, "Confidence is sexy. But he has to have reason to be confident. I'm more turned on by substance, and off by style with hollow substance."

The forty-one-year-old diagnostic technician said she wants "a man who is sure of himself. It makes no difference what he looks like on the outside. His mind is more important than his body. His body can go to pot next week, but his mind is forever."

The forty-one-year-old client service representative for a temporary help firm said, "I think looks are sexy, but I've found that a really good-looking man doesn't hold water when it comes to being sensitive, caring, and romantic. Too often they can't lower themselves to that, because they're too wrapped up in themselves. So I look at those kind, but I don't touch."

The thirty-seven-year-old accountant said, "It's sexy when he looks at me with a smile in his eyes. Not a look that is outward or suggestive, but a look that says he likes seeing me. I also find it sexy when a man talks a little softer to me than he does to everyone else."

The thirty-seven-year-old author and speaker said, "Sexiness has nothing to do with physical appearance. There are physical appearances I find very attractive, but they don't make my juices flow. My husband just lost forty pounds, and I don't love him an ounce more than when he had a pot belly."

I responded, "Then what is sexy to you?"

"His interest in me. The fact that I turn him on is a turn-on for me. His interest in pleasing me. Fun sex with him is just another play time, only without our clothes on."

A forty-three-year-old office manager from New York said, "Sexy to me is a man who is attentive and affectionate. When I'm working in the kitchen and he gives me a pat on the butt… that's sexy. Pleasing to look at for me can include a man who may be balding, or who is too thin, or a little overweight. I've found that men who have some flaw in their physical being often have worked to overcome that flaw and thereby gained inner strength. I find a man sexy who is compassionate in situations where others may not be ... like in a waitress situation. To me that shows strength, and that is sexy."

A fifty-three-year-old bookstore owner said, "Sexy equals easy going and eyes that sparkle. Look me in the eye when you talk to me. When I look some men in the eye, they melt and fade."

I had to ask, "What do you read into that?"

"'Gee, are you simply insecure, or are you trying to hide something?' His eyes are important for me if he's gonna get me thinking about sex."

The TV news photographer said, "Sexy to me is a charisma ... a feeling he projects, or a sense of character beyond being a paper cut out. I like a little shyness. And I don't go for massive muscles. That's scary, because he could hurt me."

I remarked that I found it interesting that she hadn't described a physical description of sexy, such as "tall, dark, and handsome," or the like.

"Those are *things*. I am so tired of being considered a *thing* by men, I wouldn't do that. The guys I work with invariably come back from an assignment with T & A shots of women's bodies made while covering a story. They make these clips into feature films for their private pleasure. In the coffee shop I said I was going to put together a male T & A tape for us girls. The boys were real insulted, but at least I found out where their goat was pastured. So, back in the studio, one of the cameramen was bent over, tying his shoe. I shot some film of his ass and whistled. He got real upset. I liked doing it back, because it gave them a sense of how we feel when we're treated like that. No, body parts aren't that sexy to me. I'm turned on by the inner man."

Here are random comments about what the women found sexy:

"Someone who is self-assured, has a good sense of humor, and isn't Mr. Macho."

"A sexy guy is a guy with a sense of humor ... doesn't let trivial things bother him, and isn't destroying his future with drugs."

"A decent appearance, funny, and honest eyes ... eyes that look at me are sexy."

A majority, sixty-seven percent, of women I surveyed, found a man's substance more sexy than his appearance. However, thirty-three percent were turned on more by physical appearances. Here are a few of their comments:

The twenty-seven-year-old clerical worker said, "Sexy to me

is well-built, with lots of muscle—muscles developed through physical work, rather than body building. Sexy is not a bodybuilder type. I want naturally developed muscles and dark hair."

A forty-five-year-old insurance clerk in a doctor's office said, "Sexy men are well-built with a flat stomach."

"A good body is sexy. I like a trim, well conditioned man. I want him in shape."

"A man who dresses nicely, has toned muscles, but not a jock body builder."

"Tall, dark, handsome, mustache, a little arrogant, and kind of sly. Sharp dresser. Clean cut, but not a cherry pie face look. Proud of themselves."

"A rugged, cowboy type who dresses that way."

"Slender, with clear eyes, nice teeth, nice smile, and a butt, like in the Wrangler commercial."

A forty-nine-year-old services manager in a defense plant said, "Grooming is important. Physical attributes are important. If he doesn't look good, I won't consider him further. I don't like that trait in me. I think it's a defect."

* * * * * *

This next question,

What is your definition of a loving man?

seemed so close to the previous two that I nearly eliminated it. But here, again, I discovered that women have very finely-tuned definitions.

One woman said, "A loving man is one who pays attention to all of me, not just certain parts."

The bank secretary said, "A loving man has hands that are strong and tough when working with tools or machinery, and soft and gentle when it comes to me. Soft and tender is not a weakness to him. That makes him loving."

A young paralegal said, "A loving man is caring and sincere. He thinks about me as much as he thinks about himself. He is concerned for my well-being."

The twenty-nine-year-old secretary said, "A loving man can tell when I'm down and sees through emotional guards I might put up, and then he can be honest and ask me what's really going on."

The counselor said her definition of a loving man was, "First, somebody who loves himself and is willing to receive the love of other people around him, including me. A man who thinks life is neat, who sees choices instead of victimization."

The president of a personnel pool said, "A loving man cares about flowers, ants, and flies, as well as humans. He cares about the world."

A young housewife said, "A man who cares enough to fix a meal and set a nice table ... light candles and a fire, and have rented a good movie. Someone who would once in a while make it my day. Do that for me, and he's got everything he wants from me."

The twenty-four-year-old television reporter said, "Someone who will take time for little things. Like, when I'm cooking, and he comes by and touches me, or hugs, or squeezes my hand. Someone who is easily affectionate without trying to go somewhere with it. That says so much more about how he feels about me than sex. It's more satisfying than having sex two days running. Plain unadulterated affection makes me feel good all over ... makes me like myself, and *him*. Give me genuine affection, and you'll have all the sex you can handle."

The thirty-seven-year-old parts manager said, "A loving man is a guy who loves me from the time I get up in the morning. If a man knows that, he'll get all the sex and love he wants from me. Just don't wait until around late news time to start loving or touching me, and expect me to be 'hot to trot' in five minutes. That attitude borders on sex on demand."

A thirty-year-old receptionist said she likes "little kisses on the cheek that aren't designed to catapult me into bed that instant. A guy with a tender heart, who can remove a sticker from a puppy's paw. A man who isn't afraid to cry. Those things say he's a loving man."

The lawyer said, "A caress when I least expect it. Someone who is supportive in my decisions in what I'm doing in my job. Also, a guy who appreciates what I'm doing for him, such as setting a nice table, or sewing on a button."

The forty-three-year-old retail salesperson said, "Loving and caring go hand in hand. He's got to care to love. When I had a car accident, he cried and hovered over me. He reassured our son with hugs and holding his hand. To me, his actions defined him as a caring, loving person."

The Associated Press photographer said, "A loving man does

small things on a day-to-day basis. He could forget flowers on Valentine's Day, and I'm happy as a lark if in the months before he showed an active interest in my life, and was compassionate, caring, and interested in my physical needs. Being kind, and having patience. All of those things are acts of a loving person."

The twenty-six-year-old television reporter said, "A loving man will go out of his way for my well-being. Once I tried hard to hold onto a relationship, even though I wasn't that happy with it. He sensed my unhappiness, and thank God he loved me enough to eventually let me go. *That's* a loving man."

The paralegal said, "A loving man doesn't get in a hurry for a sexual relationship before I have gotten to know him, or he has gotten to know me."

A thirty-six-year-old housewife said, "A loving man is a compassionate man, not only towards me, but to other people. If he treats me well but treats other people like dirt, he can't expect me to love, or even like, him. And compassion includes sensitivity to my sexual needs and feelings."

Some miscellaneous comments were:

"A loving man can be turned down one day for sex and not let it worry him. A loving man will understand and not feel bad toward me. He loves me just as much, knowing our time together will come. When he's that loving, I may even get horny and attack him."

"A loving man is one who wants to be with me badly enough that he will help with dishes so we can have time together. And it's not the amount of time, it's the quality. Just fifteen or twenty minutes each day to find out how I'm feeling inside ... what's on my mind."

The television news photographer said, "A loving man loves life. If he loves people and life and cares about living, learning, and growth, he's probably going to be both interesting and loving. In my opinion, he can't treat me any better than he treats himself. Also, a loving man doesn't hit little children, kick dogs, or throw cats across the room. If he did those things, I'd assume that sooner or later he'll treat me the same way."

3

Women Talk about Men and Sex

THE NEXT NINETEEN QUESTIONS are about sex. When I finished asking a woman my questions, I often wondered why she had been so open with me ... why she never flinched at what are very personal questions, such as, "Do you prefer a penis that is large or not so large?" I'll probably never know why the women answered so freely, however I can speculate.

    I was a television personality that most of them had seen for twenty years. From talking with them via a daily program, the women considered me "family." They had watched my children grow with theirs and helped bury my first born after he died at eighteen in a car-train collision. Market surveys indicated that my audience rated me at record high levels on credibility and honesty. So I came to them not as a stranger, but as a person that, by their definition, they were intimate with. Additionally, I am small... five feet three inches and 124 pounds, hardly big enough to pose a physical threat to most women. Under those conditions, sexual tension between us was minimal. That the women were mentally relaxed is reflected in their candor on very personal subjects.

The first question I asked about sex was:

On a scale of zero to ten, how important is sex to you personally? How important is sex to a man, and is there a difference for you between having sex and making love?

To women, the importance of sex rated an average of seven. These same women rated the importance of sex to their men as an average of 8.5. Sixteen percent of the women voted the other way, saying sex was more important to them than to their man. Typical comments were:

"Because I'm divorced and don't date a lot, I do have natural urges. When they hit, it's nice to have a friend I can call and say, 'Hey, it's time.' In that sense, sex is very important. However, all I get is a close feeling for just a moment. I'm searching for someone I can make love to. That's ten times more important to me."

"Just plain sex feels good for a short time, but that feeling fades pretty fast. To make love with someone gives me a feeling and a glow that lasts for a long time. It's a real sharing."

"How do you feel about playful, frolicking sex?" I asked.

"I'm not interested in sex just for the moment. I want sex that has meaning ... in other words, the caring, sharing carried from a relationship into making love. There's no law that says that can't be fun too, but the emotional satisfaction and fun are all cut from the same fabric of love. And that's the way I want it."

"My choice between sex and making love? Okay. Sex can be had with any Joe Blow to get rid of your physical need. But to make love is a whole new ball game. That's a closeness. When I make love, I don't need an orgasm to feel the closeness. The gentle, caring, touching is so important I rate that higher than anything else. Nine for making love. One for plain sex."

"I think most women got cheated on sex drive. But then, would we turn into animals if we had the same drive as men? Maybe our difference in sex drive is nature's way of identifying caring lovers from wham-bam studs. Women quickly know the difference and can then make a better long-term partner choice."

Another woman said, "At the moment, I'm in a weird time in my life. I'm twenty-one and haven't been dating for a while. Right now, sex seems pretty important to me personally ... about an eight. But six months ago, when I was dating, and sex was in my life, it was a two. Men I've known rate the importance of sex at about a ten, whether they are dating or not."

"Sex rates about a five. I want a good sex life, but if it isn't good, I won't trash an otherwise good relationship. It's a minor part of the relationship for me. I mean, if you are happy with the other twenty-three hours, that hour of sex isn't a big deal. But for him I think the importance of sex is around an eight."

One woman said, "Oh God, ten for me, and ten for him."

Another said, "I give it a ten in the importance of life. But I give only a one in allowing sex alone to control my life."

This from a forty-six-year-old: "The older I get, the more important sex gets. If it isn't there, I feel something tremendous is missing in my life."

Another said, "A hop into bed isn't all there is to sex. Sex is what goes on between you all day, or week. In church, holding little fingers has sex appeal to me ... the little touches are sex, too."

"A man and a relationship takes time I don't want to give up. I'm putting a lot of energy into painting and producing an art teaching video, and so on. I'm also trying to get my work into galleries across the country. So right now I rate sex about a three."

"Five for me, but I have to qualify that. Sex seems more important after you have had a very satisfying sexual relationship. Hormones are important on your scale, too. Remember when we were teenagers?"

The electronic maintenance person said, "It's not as important as it was earlier in my life. I've matured somewhat. I'm not as wild as even a few years ago. I don't have insecurities any more. I'm more realistic than I used to be. For me, sex is about a three."

And this from a medical records technician, "Sex is important. It's the ultimate expression. I had a marvelous, patient sex teacher. He allowed me to be myself ... no inhibitions. After I got the hang of it, we have clicked every time for thirty years. He makes it beautiful. Sex anywhere, everywhere. A most marvelous experience of my life. Early on it was about a five for me, but now it's a ten."

Our television photographer said, "Sex based on intimacy provides unequalled closeness to another human. Oh, you can feel closeness just cooking breakfast for a friend, or on a job with a co-worker. But sex is so personal and private that when it is coupled with an intimate, caring, full service relationship, I look forward to it. On the other hand, just plain animal sex, which can be intensely physical once or twice, burns me out real quick. Just plain sex makes me feel like I'm a blow up doll ... blow the doll up, and let's get it over with. That type of relationship you can have with anybody or anything, including yourself. Those sex partners are usually selfish and leave me empty and not wanting to be with them again. It's a wham-bam road to depression. Thanks, but no thanks. On the other hand, an intimate, sharing, genuinely caring relationship is special. Those elements elevate sex to a special happening, an important, worthwhile, satisfying, fulfilling, happy feeling, time after time, month after month, and year after year. If I find you honest, caring, interested in life, etc., I have difficulty resisting you sexually. Blow up doll sex is a zero. Intimate sex is a ten."

The twenty-nine-year-old secretary said, "Sex is something every living thing does. Dogs, mosquitoes, whales, dandelions. But making love is an emotional thing that includes, or leads up to, the physical act. Without emotional intimacy in the beginning, there won't be very strong emotion after the act. If it's just sex, all I get is a sore thing. Less than zero for just sex, but ten for making love."

Here is a selection of other representative comments: "Sex is a bodily function. Making love is something different ... more a very pleasant mental state. Sex, zero; making love, ten."

"Sex is about a three for me. Making love, which doesn't have to include intercourse, would be about a nine."

Further descriptions of making love were:

"Hugging, touching, rubbing your arm, rubbing lotion on your feet, kissing, snuggling. Those are real important to me."

"Sex is probably the least important part of the relationship. How he treats me, and his beliefs and values are more important."

"To eliminate sex from my life would take away a lot of excitement. Ten."

"I used to think sex was over at forty. Boy, was I dumb ... it just gets better and better. Ten."

"You can do sex in fifteen minutes, with anybody. Sex, zero. Not important at all. Making love is another ball game. It's something you do all day, every day, including taking that extra second to sneak in there and pat him on the bottom, or him pat you on the bottom. Making love begins with the day you share. Give it about a nine or ten."

One of *Parade's* female respondents to their August 1994 sex survey said, "A lot of women realize that (unless you like to be depressed afterwards) you can't separate sex from emotion. Now men are catching on too … they're figuring out that (to have a fuller sex life) emotional attachment to their partner really matters."

A fifth grade teacher defined the difference between sex and love this way: "A person's sexual expression is narrow because of the physical limits of their body. On the other hand, our ability to feel, and express, love's emotional range is boundless."

* * * * * *

How do you feel about a husband believing he is entitled to sex with you on demand?

NINETY-FOUR PERCENT of the women said, "No way." Six percent said, "Fine."

The thirty-one-year-old lawyer said, "Bull. Besides, it's a crime in most states for a husband to force his wife into sex. Some states tie it to legal separation. During a visit, if the man insists on sex, under the terms of separation, he is acting illegally. Or, if he moves back in, it is still illegal."

The counselor said, "That's like, 'Heel!' 'Speak!' 'Roll over!' … in other words, 'Do tricks!' I think that's where the term 'turning a trick' came from. That promotes the idea that a woman is property. In ancient Rome and Greece, women were not viewed as whole beings, they were considered the incubators for babies. The men loved each other. The Olympics revolved around men only.

"Woman's place was, 'More grog, wench,' or, 'Lay down, bitch … on your back." That's not about making love, that's about power. A man who today believes he is entitled to sex on demand is further back than Rome. He's still in a cave."

Other comments from the women were:

"There are women who believe they have to do it because he announces it is time. I should not have to do it when I don't want to."

"Excuse me, please. I'm not a thing. I wouldn't keep a husband like that."

"Sex on demand? I think sex is a mutual agreement."

"An ex-husband did that, and I resented it. It made me feel cheap. Even if I don't want it when he does, if he'll just work up to it, then it might be acceptable. But not just cold turkey. That's a turn-off."

"I don't like that idea. And I don't think a woman should demand sex from a man."

"I dare him to try. Demand is the key word. Asking is one thing, demanding is another."

"I think most men feel that way. I don't think it is a given, but I would try to please him all of the time. At the same time, I don't feel he is automatically entitled to it in marriage. It would not make me happy."

"I've never turned my husband down, and it's not that I feel it is my duty or an obligation. It's just that I love him and want to please him. But with my first, demanding husband, I did anything to avoid sex with him. He wasn't loving, and I hated sex with him."

"I shouldn't be made to feel guilty if I don't want to have sex. I should be able just to say no, without hiding in the headache box. I feel sex is probably a lot more important to a man at times, and that bothers me."

"I think that's an extremely self-centered opinion. Besides, it's called rape."

"As a general operating rule, I wouldn't like that worth a flip. However, I used to tell my husband that once in a while I wish he'd walk in, take the dish cloth from me, and throw me on the kitchen floor. But not as an everyday diet. I'd box him backwards."

"I'd see him as just a male animal slobbering after a bitch in heat. Listen up: I'm no animal running around in heat out in the yard. No way, Jose."

"Men tend to think that sex is a cure-all. If you had a bad day, or an ingrown toenail, migraine, no raise, rotten kids, flat tire, washing machine dumped water over the floor, and the light company is gonna' shut you off because the bill hasn't been paid ... that's not conducive to sex, or at least good sex for a woman. Men, on the other hand, think that if you get thrown to the floor and get your fuzz bumped, you'll be hunky-dory again. Crap on those kind. I want a man who can say, 'Come here and let me hold you.' Hell, even with a lot of problems, I'm willing to bump with a guy like that. So it depends on what's coming from his heart."

The motel night clerk said, "My former husband did that, and I didn't like it. One night when he'd finished and headed for the bathroom I said, 'Hey, wait a minute.' Over his shoulder he said, 'What?' I hollered, 'I want fifty dollars on the dresser.' From the bathroom he said, 'What are you talking about?' I said, 'If you're going to treat me like a whore, by God you're going to pay me like a whore.' He said he wasn't paying me a dime, so I told him in that case, in the future to just keep that thing to himself. That lasted until the next time he knocked me around." She smiled. "He's not around any more."

Following are some views of the six percent of women in my survey who thought sex on demand was acceptable:

"I have no problem with that. I believe he's entitled."

"I think it is okay."

"I've never refused a husband, and I feel great about that."

"I'd probably like it. But then, I've been divorced and celibate for six months, so that may be just my present biological state. Later I might not like that."

*   *   *   *   *   *

In a gym class locker and shower room, there probably isn't a male who hasn't silently compared the size of his penis with those of his classmates. And most males probably rate their manhood or sexiness according to their penis size. But how important is penis size to a woman? To find out, I asked:

How important is the size of a man's penis? Do you prefer large or not so large?

SEVENTY-SIX PERCENT of the women said they preferred an average-sized penis or less. The other twenty-four percent said they preferred a large penis.

The television reporter said, "It doesn't have to be massive. I don't want him to be tiny, either. If he's an average endowed man, that's just fine. It's not a big deal. As long as he can satisfy me, size isn't that important."

The bank secretary said, "I don't like real large. I dated a guy one time and he was so large he really hurt me. It's more what he does with what he has to work with. If he knows how to handle a woman, he doesn't need a large penis. Besides, it's not really how long it is, it's how thick it is."

The television camera person said, "Size is pretty important. I ran across a man who was huge. I couldn't possibly handle him, and I said, 'No thanks, I can't do it.' Then there was this other guy who was really peanut sized, bless his heart. But we did fine. It's mostly the way it's used. But too long can be painful. Even if I really like the person, if sex is painful, I can't relax and enjoy it. Too large is a turn off. It hurts like getting hit on the head with a hammer. My insides hurt if it's too large."

The counselor said, "It depends on how inventive he is with other parts of his anatomy. Most women reach orgasm through finger stimulation of their clitoris. Or if he's willing to do oral sex, his size is even less important. If it is bigger, that's nice, but that's not a requirement."

The bank purchasing agent said, "That's a ridiculous question. It makes no difference. I can make love and never have sex organ contact. As long as he kisses me and hugs me and makes me feel important and loved, I can have love-making without his penis. It's a miracle that women put up with men in their first twenty years. It takes men so long to become good lovers."

A thirty-year-old quality control clerk for a cellular phone company said, "Not so large, please. It's more important what he does with it than what he's got. I can have sex with a guy who has a large penis and not enjoy it. He may enjoy, but I'm not going to get much out of it. Most men don't understand that."

Random comments were:

"The skill with which he uses it is more important than size."

"Large or not so large, I don't care."

"I prefer large, but as far as importance, size isn't where it's at."

The motel night clerk said, "If it reaches from him to me, it's long enough. And if it won't reach one way, I'll help him make it reach another. What matters is what's coming to me through the vibrations of a man's heart and his mind. It's hard to lay there stark naked without getting the truth. A woman has a sixth sense that alerts her to a man who is not on the up and up with her, or if he's just shooting from the hip. Women hear anything before the sexual encounter but after it's all over, that's when the truth comes out. If he's carrying shadows or skeletons from former encounters, or if he's got problems in his head, that's when a woman is really tuned in. She'll sense if he's genuine or just trying to shovel a load at her. The size of his penis won't help one way or another."

* * * * * *

I think most men who have ejaculated into a female wonder how she feels at her moment, and how her sensation compares to his. In hopes of getting insight on how her moment feels, I asked,

What do you get from sex?

A FIFTY-TWO-YEAR-OLD TEACHER from Alabama said, "I don't know, but when I get it, my friends say, 'Oh, where did your wrinkles go?' It's a physical thing. After good sex, I feel a whole lot better about myself. I feel touched. I feel known. I feel seen. I feel like someone has trusted me enough to let me in, to let me get that close. It's incredibly special. It's more than just the physical release … it's the freedom of not having to hold back who I am, of being able to let go totally. To surrender to that whole energy flow. I think we're both surrendering something. It's so incredibly relaxing, but it also has a lot to do with being accepted. Deeply accepted. I don't think it works that way for most men, and that's a pity. But that's what I get from sex."

The services manager in a defense plant said, "From sex I get physical relief, and the feeling that I'm attractive to that person, and he wants sex with me. From making love I get all of the above, with icing on the cake. I think men believe they can solve a lot of problems in the bedroom. I don't feel that way. It's difficult for me to be loving after we've had an argument and I'm angry. For me to enjoy lovemaking, other aspects of the relationship must be good. Instant sex is okay no more than twenty-five percent of the time. Making love, I want seventy-five percent of the time."

The thirty-year-old quality control clerk for a cellular phone company said, "I get physical enjoyment from sex. Making love, however, is more emotional … there's physical in it, but it's more on an emotional level. It's more of a gut feeling. There's more sharing in making love than in sex. Physically, anyone can have sex. Making love's not as easy, but worth it."

I then asked, "What is your scale rating on making love, compared with plain sex?"

"Making love is a ten, and plain sex is a five," she replied.

"To him, sex?"

"Probably pretty high. I'd say a nine."

"For him, making love?"

"For your average John Doe, five or six, because he doesn't know the difference between the two."

"In an ongoing sexual relationship with one person, isn't it possible that there would be times for frolicking, fun sex, and times for making love?"

"You can't start out making love. In the beginning, all my

husband and I did was frolic, controlled by unique places, the mood we were in, etc. Making love developed with time, as we got to know each other. Part of that was because I had bad sexual experiences before. I was molested as a child by one of my stepfathers, and by my real father. I had negative feelings about my present husband, because when we first had sex, I had been married, and he was playing around. I held back, feeling like there were things that I wasn't doing, or couldn't do, or wouldn't provide. You can make love without an orgasm and feel just as fulfilled as if you'd had plain sex. There are different types of fulfillment. They are both good, and both have their place, but they're not the same thing."

Another woman said that sex gives her "a completeness. It's the highest physical event you can experience. If I compared my life to ice cream and whipped cream, the feeling I get from sex would be the cherry on top. It's the closest I'll ever be able to get to him, because you open yourself up for sex."

The electronics repair person said, "If I'm feeling insecure, then sex reinforces my belief that, God, I'm not haggy looking, or that I am acceptable to someone. And it's a bonding."

The cosmetologist said, "I get communication from sex. It's the highest level of communication there is."

The TV camera-person said, "About all I get from sex is sore. I get more satisfaction from the intimacy that occurs with the process. It seems like so many of my relationships have boiled down to just sex, and all I get from it is an empty feeling. After blatantly sexual episodes I was more lonely than ever, and it was obvious he felt nothing inside. There was certainly nothing shared by either of us. That kind of sex is so unfulfilling, it's not worth bothering with. I ache for some loving, some caring, sharing, holding, talking, caressing ... all of the fulfilling, neat, intimate things that either go before, or at least with, the actual sex are the most important aspects to me. I find that basically men are either damned lazy at lovemaking or they don't give a shit. I find it hard to believe they don't know how, especially after all their macho crap. There's not a giving or a sharing or caring. To most of them, it's just an act that gets their balls off. I've heard guys joking about, 'Oh God, she wanted some foreplay.' If I'd known in the beginning that all he cared about was to get his rocks off and go to sleep, I'd have kept my pants on. Men don't understand—and don't seem interested in understanding—that men and women are different that way. I think sometimes men just use women as a little fancier device than their fist for masturbation. Give me a break. I accused a man of that once. He was highly insulted, but insulted or not, it was the truth ... and he knew it. That's why he was insulted ... that I picked up on it. I told him if he wanted to masturbate, do it somewhere else other than inside me. I don't need that. Of course that didn't help the relationship a whole hell of a lot. But I'd gotten to a point where I couldn't stand it any more. This was the guy loaded with potential, but he was in so much fear of touching. Intimacy scared him so badly that he couldn't touch me in a loving way. At one point, I asked him if he'd just hold me for a little bit ... thinking maybe if I asked, it would happen. Well, stupid me. Instead of holding me, he freaked out, thinking he was less adequate because I had to ask him. He had a major ego problem. I mean, male egos are real delicate. But if you're not getting what you want and need, and he isn't willing to learn, I say show him the door. I stuck it out way too long. I thought he had potential."

"Was it you who felt he had potential," I asked, "or was it him doing a selling job on his potential?"

"It was me thinking it. It was me not looking at reality. I kept thinking that underneath all his fears and barriers there was a person who was caring and loving and affectionate, but who wasn't capable of showing it. I wasn't able to bring it out, and it was real frustrating. It taught me that we really can't change people, that a person is what they are. If they choose to change, that's their choice, but we can't change them. That's why it's so important to know somebody a long time before you get involved, because once sex happens, there's this unspoken possession bit that occurs. From there on, my giving him sex seemed to stop his development of intimacy. So while he is regularly getting his rocks off, the relationship for me gets sicker and sicker, and my twat gets sorer and sorer. I don't need that."

A thirty-seven-year-old environmentalist said, "Intercourse gives me emotional nurturing as well as physical enjoyment. I get a feeling of euphoria from knowing that I'm loved. Sex is one of the blessings that God has given me. Sex nurtures my soul as well as my body."

The TV anchor person said, "From sex, I get physical satisfaction, maybe. When it's over, I feel a lack of emotional satisfaction and have emotional guilt. I'm Catholic and have never been open about casual sex. It doesn't make me feel very good. Sex for sex's sake might feel good at the moment, but it makes me feel like shit afterwards. As for making love, it's a feeling that warms you inside. It's a secure feeling that comes from knowing you've just made love to someone you love and can trust, and who cherishes you. It's a warm glow that makes me feel good about myself. If the love is good and the lovemaking is there, it lasts. It extends. Sex can extend too, but in a very negative way. Making love extends in a positive way. To be honest with you, I think we judge ourselves by the social standard of 'nice girls just don't do that.' If we do, we're totally guilt ridden. I think a guy lays there and thinks, 'That was great,' and has no guilt or problem at all. However, all guys are not necessarily like that."

"Tell John Doe what percentage of the time you feel comfortable with frolicking sex, and lovemaking sex," I requested.

"That's hard to put a number on. When I feel good about someone, it's just spur of the moment. Some days you look at each other and a silent message passes saying, 'We're gonna make love, and it's gonna be good, romantic.' Or sometimes, you can be just fooling around, and the next thing you know …"

"Give John Doe a majority then …"

"I want romantic lovemaking slightly more times than frolicking sex."

The Santa Fe shop owner said, "I get physical gratification and relaxation, plus an emotional bonding that can't be had any other way. I get exactly what I want. You get what you want, and you get what you give. If you're with the right person and are willing to give, you'll get even more back. Right there is the difference between making love and having sex."

The thirty-five-year-old secretary said, "I get enjoyment from sex. I also get physical companionship, and if the guy is smart about it, the intimacy that goes with it. From making love I get a closeness that equals no other. There's a bond that most people want. Sex is just physical, but making love is deeper. Making love gives me a glow that lights my being … my life."

The client service rep for a temporary help firm said, "From my first husband I didn't get a lot from sex. We were young, and kind of mechanical. He had this macho façade, and couldn't make me feel comfortable about his feelings. What I want from sex is closeness and security. If feedback from him tells me I'm performing well, I feel secure about our relationship. When I have pleased my partner and let him know he has pleased and satisfied me, I feel our relationship is secure, and that neither of us needs anyone else."

An alterations shop owner said, "Sex gives me peace of mind. I feel like it puts harmony in my life. Sex frees my mind to do other, bigger things, like making money, tending to my daughter, visiting relatives, donating my time somewhere."

The author/speaker said, "Sex is fun with somebody I'm in a long term relationship with. I love the physical stimulation ... it's tremendous ... wonderful. I can't imagine anything better. Eating is the only thing that comes close. Sex is a phenomenal physical experience, and also fun. A good time for laughing, intimacy, conversation, silliness. Sex is a whole lot of stuff. Closeness. The intimacy isn't strictly sexual, it's also an emotional high. On the other hand, with someone I'm not sure of, it's just physical, and not nearly as much fun."

The bank executive secretary said, "From sex, I want a reassurance that I am attractive and beautiful and that he wants to give to me something that can only be had through genuine love. I want to be able to live my fantasies. That's what I want. I get all of that with my present husband, for the first time in my life, and I'm forty-eight now. We've been married six years, and our sex life just gets better and better. We dated two years. From a previous husband, I got nothing ... no climax for the whole seven years I was married to him. I kept searching for it and wanting it, but no go. I had three kids." She paused, and continued. "My second husband was a 'Nam vet. I thought I had found what I didn't have with my first husband. He was a better lover, but he gave me nothing emotionally to hang on to. He was wrapped up in himself, a self out of the Vietnam war. He couldn't hold a job, couldn't support us ... survived two tours in 'Nam and then as a civilian died of a massive heart attack. My third husband was an older man who'd never had a family. I brought three kids. It was not emotionally a satisfactory marriage. He gave me what I needed financially, but having financial things and no emotional support coupled to a mediocre sex life left me empty. Once in a while I got lucky in bed, but not often. It got to the point where I was disillusioned over our sex life, and that created other problems. Then we had a huge fight that completely changed my attitude toward him. There is one thing men don't understand. Love to a woman is like a flower garden ... you must weed it, cultivate it, take care of it, make sure it gets lots of sun and lots of rain to keep that garden growing. If you don't, it is possible to kill what a woman feels for you. You may not realize that. A man must nurture a woman to keep her going all the time. That's what a man needs to know. A woman's responsibility is to keep the life and love flowing in the family. If she ever loses her enthusiasm for the marriage, it's doomed. You can't afford to let her lose her enthusiasm. You must keep nurturing her. The more you nurture her, the more she'll nurture you. It's a never ending circle, like a wedding ring ... it keeps going and going and blossoming and flowing. If you kill the respect she has for you, the love dies. It's like pulling a flower up by its roots and throwing it aside ... it will die. Men don't understand that just because a woman is in love with you, it doesn't mean she will always be, unless you take care of the love she gives. You must nurture and take care of it. If you don't, you'll kill it. The last big fight I had with him killed it. I got in the car and drove around a couple of hours. When I came back, it was gone. I didn't feel the same. I packed my things and moved out, and it was over. My present husband allows me to be all that my potential and our circumstances will allow me to be. Rather than smother me, he nurtures me. I just love him for that, and I get everything I want from sex with him."

Random comments:

"I get a lot of pleasure."

"Sex rounds out the rest of my life."

"It gives me a feeling of self worth. Makes me feel real important to him."

"It makes me feel like a female, and a woman ought to feel like a woman."

"I get orgasm. That's how I spell relief. O-R-G-A-S-M."

*   *   *   *   *   *

Logically, it seemed my next question should be:

What do you want from sex?

THE CPA SECRETARY said, "Good sex is about ninety percent mental and ten percent physical. From good sex I feel important and on top of the world. I don't relate to a sexual feeling, I relate to an emotional feeling. For me, sex and making love are the same. I think a *caring* man gets the same feelings."

The TV news camera person said, "There are two different kinds of sex for me. There is the purely physical, where I simply get physical satisfaction. Other times, not as many as I want, sex is an expression of sharing love with the man. Then it's like a statement, 'I love you.' But ninety-eight percent of the time, I'm sorry to say, the guy gives me only purely physical ... he just wants his rocks off. And sometimes I only get a sore twat, especially if he's drunk."

A thirty-two-year-old secretary asked, "Does your question, 'what do I want from sex,' include sex without intercourse?"

"Define a sexual experience *without* intercourse," I requested.

"Heavy petting, French kissing, fondling my breasts, fingering me, and/or giving me oral sex. If he's skilful, he can satisfy my needs with those activities. After he's done the above, he can do anything to me he wants. He can even stop there and cuddle me, or go home, or turn on the light and read."

"You mean stop, as without proceeding to intercourse?"

"Yes. I don't need anything more." She laughed. "HE might, but I don't."

A counselor said, "A relationship that includes genuine lovemaking builds a bonding. Anybody can have sex. Making love is an art. When you make love, you are more interested in making your partner feel good. When we make love, if he ends up with that special smile on his face, then I feel like Rocky, because I'm more interested in making him feel good, or vice versa ... it works both ways ... it takes a little bit longer for me. My mother says, 'Men are like microwaves and women are like crockpots.' That's the difference. You can't make love without having had sex or playful sex, because making love is an art. It's unique in and of the two people who are doing it. I think you have to have the frolicking sex before you can reach the making love part because, when you make love, you usually don't have an itinerary going, saying, 'I want #1, #3, and a little bit of #7.' Instead, you start out and you just take your time. Making love needs time and no threat of interruption. Usually, making love is preceded by anything from sitting and drinking wine by the fire to rubbing you down with lotion after you get out of the bathtub or shower together. It's more of a bonding process than sex. What I get from sex is usually just a plain and simple release."

"Is it safe to say that you want more of an atmosphere for making love than for sex?" I asked.

"Yeah ... I want candlelight, perfume, wine, and soft music. That's the part that makes it different, the atmosphere."

"In just straight sex, would it be fair to say that it's okay for you to pursue your own feeling?"

"Yes, in frolicking sex. In making love, you're more concerned for your partner. Sex itself is really very self-centered, whereas making love is more of an effort of the two people involved."

A single, forty-two-year-old, department store salesperson said, "I expect from sex something better than what I had with my first husband. I haven't yet experienced what I expect ... that wonderful feeling I hear about that is supposed to make you feel so good. I think if I had a partner who would talk to me, let me talk to him, and listen to me it would be okay. If I say 'this hurts,' or 'that feels good,' I expect him to hear that. I expect him to not continue an event if I tell him it hurts. I realize that must be said in a way that doesn't offend, or sound aggressive, or blaming. I've read all the books about this, and I expect him to listen. But it has to be right. Like the other day, a twenty-nine-year-old propositioned me. I said no, and he asked if I ever had sex for the pure pleasure of it. I said 'No, that my head and my heart must go together, and if they don't, it's not right for me. If it's not right for me, isn't it selfish of you to think it would be right for you?'" She laughed. "Talk about being used. Well, anyway, he said he could do it for the sheer pleasure. I told him to find someone else."

The twenty-seven-year-old clerical worker said, "Sex only gives me a release and satisfies my physical needs. I want lovemaking, which satisfies both my physical and emotional needs."

"What is the release you get from sex?" I asked.

"Tension. If I'm under a lot of stress, sex relieves that stress."

The counselor said, "What I want from sex is to make love. From making love, I get an expanded sense of myself. I also feel connected with somebody else, not so alone. I also feel I'm acknowledged and invited into a dimension of life that is wonderful. It's a part of what being a person is about. It's wonderful."

"What about frolicking sex?"

"Lots of that. Sexuality is where the child in us can come out. That doesn't have to be a divine experience. It can be just look and taste and hold and play. And a lot of 'let's run off into the back room while the kids watch cartoons.' Lots and lots of play. It doesn't have to be planned. It's just fun. When people hear the word, there's a caveman mentality about it. 'Lay down, I think I love you.' Frolicking sex is fun. If you let yourself hear, there's this blend of universe stuff, this other stuff of the two-of-us-seeing-one-another, and a big hunk of stuff that's just playful. And there are times when sex happens when you feel bad ... 'Let me make you feel better.' And there's deep sex, and sometimes sex is a power exercise ... 'Because I say so ... now!'"

The forty-four-year-old radio ad salesperson said, "Orgasms are important to me ... the physical deal. That's what I want."

"What does orgasm give you?" I asked.

"A wonderful, euphoric feeling through an intense release. Intensity depends on how long it's been. At other times, orgasm comes from a culmination of a lot of other things. And sometimes, to be crude, it's like scratching an itch. It's just 'gotta be done.'"

Random comments:

"Sex is a form of communication that I like and want."

"I get closeness. A bonding. It can also be a used feeling ... a wham-bam thing."

"Sex can be a deadly experience in this age of AIDS. It can dig your grave."

"I get a feeling of total satisfaction and closeness with my man. I feel like I'm part of him. That's what I want ... that closeness and companionship."

"I want closeness, and sometimes I get that, but sometimes I don't. Sometimes I feel used, like I am only a thing under him ... that anything warm would serve him just as well."

"I get nothing from sex ... absolutely nothing. From making love I get emotional satisfaction, a feeling of happiness, joy, and a feeling of comfort."

"From making love I get a warm, glowing, snuggly, good feeling that lasts. I want that glowy feeling."

* * * * * *

Do you have a preference as to who should initiate sex?

THE CLIENT SERVICE REP for a temporary help firm said, "I like the man to initiate a majority of the time, because that makes me feel desired and wanted. It's also a turn-on. But I also know a man likes a woman to initiate sometimes, for the same reasons. So, we need to hit a happy medium where neither is afraid to start sex. A man told me that men let women initiate sex because they don't want to feel the pain of rejection. It's difficult for them when a woman says no. Therefore, men tend to sit back and let the women initiate. But when that becomes a habit, the woman begins to feel he doesn't desire her. If that happens, her eyes may cast looks at other men."

The forty-six-year-old marriage counselor said, "I think there has to be a little more than half each way ... say fifty-three percent for each partner. In other words, each has to do more than their half. Depending on what ages they are, some years it may be the man more, and in other years, the woman seems to work best. And don't base starting something on, 'just because I asked you last time, it's your turn to ask me.' No keeping score. Base it on whoever feels like going for it.

"Initiating is touchy. It has to be both, and not every time just saying you want to go to bed. That's fine once in a while, but not as a matter of habit. A man should be sensitive enough that he shouldn't have to ask ... just make some moves. Aside from those once in a while spur of the moment deals, sex should be worked up to over a period of hours.

"I have preferences, but I know what actually happens. I think a woman should be allowed to initiate. But I don't think socially she is really allowed. Unfortunately, women play these games where we have to sit and hold back while we're thinking, 'God, I wish he'd jump my bones'. I wish I could initiate it. When sitting across the room, I wish I could say, 'Hey, honey, want to fool around?' And if he wants to, for him to jump and say, 'Let's do it.' Unfortunately, convention says I have to hold back. I wish convention said it was okay for me to go for it, without any game playing."

Random comments:

"There are ways that a woman can initiate without taking anything from a man's ego. Women are sly things ... we can do subtle little things to get things started, and then just go with the flow."

"Women seem more willing to angle for sex early in the evening, or in the morning. Men seem to lean toward the evening."

"I think a man likes when a woman is turned on and goes for him."

"I think it should be whoever is in the mood."

"Who starts sex should always vary."

"Makes no big difference, but I won't want to be the one all the time. I want him to initiate some too. Hopefully, fifty-fifty."

"My husband would rather it be me more often, and that's fine with me."

"I like it better when my husband does. That way I really know his feelings, without having to guess."

"I hate to admit this, but I like it better when the guy starts it."

"The way I was raised, and the way I was influenced by movies, it was always romantic and wonderful that the man initiated, with music in the background, and so on. Unfortunately, that isn't reality ... that's only in the movies, or in your mind. The more secure I get with myself the more I think it ought to be a mutual deal. There's this wonderful scene in Out of Africa, where Redford comes home and Streep comes in from the field. Both begin undressing each other and kissing and spinning around. It's obvious that both want to, and that's the way it should be. Where each wants the other so much, they help each other undress. No one started it, it was a both deal."

* * * * * *

How important is the "big O" to women? I asked:

On a scale of zero to ten, how important is orgasm?

THE AVERAGE OF THE IMPORTANCE of orgasm to the women was 6.6. Twenty-one percent of the women rated the importance of orgasm for them a "ten." Six percent gave that event a "zero." The range of answers was from "zero" to "twelve."

The television news photographer said, "Eighty to ninety percent of the time it's real important. Depends on the circumstance. Guys think they'll get blue balls if they don't get their rocks off to relieve pain caused by stimulation and tension. But if you frustrate a woman to that point, we get very painful too. If he doesn't care enough, and is only interested in himself, and leaves me out there on a limb, oh man, I'm hung over for days. I get resentful, angry, grouchy, and bitchy. But there's another side to that coin.

"There are times when I don't care about an orgasm ... if I'm tired, or don't feel all that great, or if my hormones just aren't up. It's my choice, and it's usually when I'm not particularly hot to trot. *But*, by God, if he gets me into a heat of passion and leaves me high and dry, that's when it's tough. I get resentful. But the funny part is, when he leaves me high and dry, if he'll just hold me and talk to me and caress me, and spend some time with me, rather than roll over and snore, it's okay."

One of the "tens" said, "If I'm going to make love, I need to complete it. Otherwise, I feel empty. But my mental state has a lot to do with it. With my first husband, we only had sex. I tried so hard for an orgasm, and *never* had one. Now, I don't even have to work at it, it just washes over me. It's easy as pie. The difference is, we make love."

The marriage counselor, who rated orgasm for her between "nine and twelve" said, "When I was younger it wasn't important, about a two." She paused. "May I make a speech to John Doe about female orgasm?"

"Please do."

"It's unfortunate that in our culture, boys and girls are taught that it's not nice to touch themselves. Mothers don't encourage masturbation by their sons or daughters. But mothers seem to forget that boys must touch their penis when they go to the bathroom. So, boys automatically become familiar with themselves, and cultures seem to accept that. On the other hand, because of the way they're constructed, girls don't become familiar with themselves as easily as boys. Therefore, compared with boys, there aren't many girls masturbating. As a result, a lot of women come into a relationship not knowing what gives them an orgasm. Not only that, a lot of their mothers never even had one, so they are little help. But boys come into a relationship knowing full well what to expect from sex, and how to get it. Problem with the boys is, most of their experience before they got with a girl had to be in the dark and quick. They did themselves fast and got it over with, so as not to get caught. Girls have had none of that. So, we have an unawakened girl, and the awakened boy who has been going off as fast as he could. Put them together, and it's a nightmare for her. She doesn't know what to tell him, because she doesn't know. To make it worse, many boys try things on her they've seen in porno movies, which are horrible sex education. They seem to be made by people from outer space. But slowly, a lot of kids today are learning how to touch each other, and how to talk. For help, I recommend a couple of books by a talented sex therapist, Lonnie Barbach. One is *Pleasures: Women Write Erotica* (HarperCollins). *Pleasures* speaks to what women say about sensual, sexual, pleasurable things. Another Barbach book, *Erotic Interludes* (HarperCollins), is written by women about women's fantasies. Books written by men are pretty useless because men haven't understood women. Men can write about *male* erotica, but few know beans about female erotica. My husband, bless his heart, tried to do things to me that he thought would enhance my pleasure. I was a sexual infant, and so was he. There was no way I could do much of that sexy playful kind of stuff. We worried a lot about getting pregnant, which we did. A screaming baby takes the pizzazz out of a relationship. In fact, it takes about four years for a marriage to stabilize. Few of us had a relationship that long before we threw babies at it. That rocked the boat before we even had a chance to know each other, or our own bodies. I instruct female clients to buy a vibrator, and get another of Barbach's books, *For Yourself: Fulfillment of Female Sexuality* (North American Library/Dutton). Another Barbach book is *For Each Other: Sharing Sexual Intimacy* (Doubleday & Company), which I recommend to couples. It has one-two-three kinds of stuff about touching and holding, and sensuality from places where women and men have a common language. Any or all of these books might help a woman understand more who she is, and also help a man understand her. A word to women regarding masturbation: once you teach yourself how to have an orgasm, you can then teach someone else to give that to you, in wonderful ways you can't, and ways that are a lot more fun than by yourself. Remember, 'A joy shared is a joy doubled.' Speech over, and good luck, guys. Getting smarter about your woman's female parts is worth the effort."

A secretary said of orgasm, "His is more important than mine because it is so much easier for a man. My orgasm depends more on the whole day it takes to build me to the point of wanting it. The previous twenty or thirty minutes have less impact on me, and therefore less of a desire for me to have orgasm. Those times, it is more important for me to make sure he is fulfilled than me."

A housewife said, "Orgasm isn't that important. But the afterplay is. The little stuff afterwards is more important to me than my orgasm. I sure don't want a guy who turns over on his back and starts snoring. That's a bit much. Give me some loving afterwards. I'll not only be fine, but I'll be back for more."

The forty-four-year-old purchasing agent from New York said, "Orgasm is important to me, but if we make love and my body isn't tuned in, it's okay not to have an orgasm. It's the closeness that counts. It's being with that person. The hugging and caressing suit me just fine."

The forty-two-year-old owner of a woman's clothing store said, "Orgasm is overrated with me. Sex is more than a physical feeling. Sex is an emotional commitment that gives rise to a feeling that lasts a long time throughout the day and beyond. The feeling I get gives a glow to my life. Orgasm comes, and then is gone. But the glow shines in my daily life. I give orgasm about a five. Lasting glow gets a twenty."

The doctor's wife said, "With my first husband, I never had an orgasm, because we never made love. We merely had sex, which was often violent and hurtful. Mentally, I hurt too, because we didn't have that sharing. I think I hurt more from that than from lack of an orgasm."

Here are selected comments women made about their orgasms:

"I enjoy orgasm, but if the sex is done right, with love, caring, and consideration, orgasm isn't as important. From lots of touching and holding and kissing and body feeling, I get ample gratification without an orgasm."

"I've never not had one, so I don't know how I'd react if I didn't."

"Orgasm for me is a four or five. It's not the most important thing I get out of it anyway. The sharing, joy, closeness and tenderness ... that's what I want."

"Zero for me on orgasm. That's not why I make love. I make love for the closeness."

"Give it a four. I can have good sex without an orgasm."

"Orgasm is important, between an eight and ten. But if it doesn't happen, I'm not going to throw my body over a cliff."

"If you're going to make love, you may as well do it right. Ten for me."

"Two. I can have good sex without having an orgasm."

"If a man doesn't honestly try to firing me to it and isn't even tender, but has gone off on his own trip, that's the last time."

"For a man to help a woman have an orgasm means a lot to her soul."

Obviously, sex encompasses a lot more for a woman than just orgasm. Women seem to have a wider range of pleasure and enjoyment, a range that includes deeper, more spiritual meaning than for many men.

* * * * * *

I think most men worry about their female partner having an orgasm. I also believe many men feel responsible for her orgasm, and if they "fail her," they feel their sexual prowess has been diminished, or even threatened. I asked the women:

When you fail to have orgasm, what percentage of the failure do you assign to your partner?

THE RADIO ADVERTISING SALESPERSON said, "I don't fail to have an orgasm, but if I did, it would be my fault. It can be his fault if he isn't cooperative, but I'm not going to find myself in that kind of relationship. I did once, and I won't repeat it."

The doctor's wife said, "Not his fault. If my day has been difficult and stressful, I may not want an orgasm. The hugging and kissing and caressing that goes with sex is satisfying to me at those times."

Our forty-one-year-old diagnostic technician said, "None. It's up to the woman whether she is going to have an orgasm or not. If she doesn't, men wonder what happened … what did he do wrong? Why didn't she come? Well, dear, you did nothing wrong. Orgasm comes only from me. Don't get the idea that just because I didn't have an orgasm that I didn't enjoy it. Men are too hung up on that."

The twenty-nine-year-old paralegal said, "I always have an orgasm. But if he gets in a hurry and doesn't give me time, then it's as much his fault as it is mine. My body is like a musical instrument. If he wants to be a good musician or a lousy musician, that's up to him, but my orgasm is mine. It depends a lot on how we play each other."

The twenty-seven-year-old office clerk said, "There are times when orgasm isn't important to me, like when I'm tired or my mood is not so high. Then the closeness is fine. When orgasm is important to me, I would say he is about twenty percent of the equation."

The forty-five-year-old teacher said, "Sometimes I may not have an orgasm because I'm too tired or worried about something in my life. Then it's my problem, not his. Most of my orgasms have to do with me."

The bank purchasing agent said, "This is something men don't understand. They think that if a woman fails to have an orgasm, it's his fault. That's not true. Women's chemical makeup is so different that it may just be our chemistry was wrong at the time. Maybe our hormones weren't clicking. For me, sometimes it's as if my mind is saying, 'Gosh, I'd sure like to have an orgasm,' but my body isn't cooperating. Sometimes my body just isn't in sync with my mind, and there's nothing he can do about that. No, my orgasm isn't his problem."

The Santa Fe shop owner said, "Sometimes things are going on with me that shut down my libido. In that case, I take full responsibility. Other times, maybe he doesn't really know much about a woman's physiology and needs some 'how to.'"

The cellular phone company quality clerk said, "Basically, a woman is responsible for satisfying herself, just like a man is responsible for himself. If she doesn't get what she wants, she should speak up, grab a hand, or give him a clue."

The counselor said, "It depends on how he talks about it with me. If we talk quietly and intelligently I'm less concerned, and only need somebody to support me. My orgasm is my orgasm. But if he's just going wham-bam when I've said I need more holding and touching, and he ignores that, gets his rocks off, and goes to sleep, I'm going to be mad. I still think it's pretty much my deal. If I want an orgasm, I need to go off by myself and take care of that in whatever way I need."

The television anchorwoman said, "I don't have an orgasm easily. When I don't, I fault him for not concentrating on me enough. The guy who satisfies me is the guy who really concentrates on me. If he is loving and caring, concerned for my feelings, and has fire and passion, then it's easier for me to let go. But he's got to love concentrating on me. If I don't have an orgasm, I give him about eighty percent of the responsibility."

Additional comments were:

"A lot depends on his skill, and how comfortable he makes me. I'd give him about fifty percent of the deal."

"Maybe five percent of the effort is his ... the rest is mine."

"All of the problem is his, because if I don't have orgasm, it's because he didn't take the time to show me he is more interested in *me* than just my body parts."

"I don't care if I have an orgasm or not, so long as he talks gently to me."

"Fifty percent is his, and fifty mine. It's not all his fault."

"Low percentage for him. The only time would be when he just wasn't interested in me and my part of it. Twenty percent for him."

"His part of my orgasm is about two percent. It's more my business than his."

"None for him. It doesn't matter if I do or don't. It's all the feelings combined. The touching, and all that, is more important to me."

* * * * * *

Allow me to explain how this next question came about. At the end of each interview, I invited the women to suggest any questions she thought should be added to my list. When I made that offer to interviewee #74, she said, "You didn't ask anything about oral sex."

After I regained my composure, I asked, "Do you mean you all would talk openly with me about that?"

Her answer was, "Try us, Buster."

On the spot, she and I devised the question:

How do you feel about giving oral sex to a man, and how do you feel about receiving oral sex from a man?

SINCE ONLY TWENTY-SEVEN of the one hundred women remained to be interviewed, that is the total number of respondents for this question. Of the twenty-seven, one declined to answer. Another had no oral sex experience.

Of the twenty-five women with oral sex experience, seventy-six percent said they liked both giving and receiving. Sixteen percent liked to give only, but not receive. Eight percent said they liked to receive, but not to give oral sex. I have selected the following answers to represent the women's views.

"In most circumstances, giving it to a man is fine. As for getting it, in some circumstances it's nice, others not."

"What circumstances?" I asked.

"It just has to be the right time."

"I like it fine both ways. But I think older people feel differently. I'm forty-five."

"Oral sex is fine, and fun. But it's not fine and fun if it's all just his way. Since most women reach orgasm by stimulation of their clitoris, oral sex given to a woman is delightful. It took a lot of growing up for me to be at ease with oral sex. When I was younger, I felt my own body was yucky and icky, but that has changed with time."

"I enjoy giving oral sex to a man, but nowadays it would have to be with someone I have known a long time, and know really well. I sure don't want AIDS."

"If it's someone I love and care about, giving him oral sex is the natural thing to do. To have him do it to me is not natural."

"Giving oral sex is the same as making love. There is an art to it. Your whole purpose when you give oral sex is for him to be fulfilled. That's how I get my gratification."

"How do you feel about receiving?" I inquired.

"With my present husband, it's the same. Normally, I think men give it because they feel it is expected more than because they want to give pleasure. A lot of men don't even know how to give pleasure that way. But, there are those precious souls who want to do it for their woman. Like I said, there's an art to doing it. If you don't know, then practice is about the only way you can learn. Oral sex is unique from woman to woman, just like each man is unique. I feel that in marriage, it's a vital part."

"I simply adore both. Truth is, I probably enjoy getting it more than giving it."

"Giving it in love making, I don't mind. I don't enjoy it, but I do not mind it either. I will go out of my way to please an honest lover. That's what love making is all about ... pleasing each other, not just yourself. So if that's important to him, it's important to me. Receiving is important, too ... very important."

"Just dating, no way. In marriage, it's fine."

"Giving it is okay, but I don't like to receive it. Not many years back, oral sex didn't even come up."

"I enjoy giving oral sex to a man because all the men I've known absolutely love it, therefore I enjoy it, because I know they do. I don't enjoy receiving oral sex."

"I don't particularly like either one."

"Me giving that to a man? More power to you ... ha ha."

"I don't like giving, but I like receiving ... aren't I selfish?"

One other woman pointed out that, for her, oral sex was not confined to genitalia, but included sucking nipples and breasts. "Two minutes on my breasts is worth twenty minutes of caressing and touching elsewhere." She paused. "Want to know a how a man can really send a woman into orbit?"

Of course I did. "Sure."

"During oral sex, treat her clitoris, which is her miniature penis, exactly as a man likes to have oral treatment of his penis." She drew a breath, "That means suck on her miniature penis, and apply your tongue where you like application. Ten seconds of that should have her screaming in agonized ecstasy."

I was amazed at the ease and openness with which the women discussed what I considered a delicate subject. Their answers taught me that most women will talk with a man about anything. Apparently all we need do is to talk with her.

* * * * * *

Our next question stood out as one of the easiest for the women to answer. It was:

If you had to give up hugging and caressing FOREVER, or sex FOREVER, which would you give up? The key word is FOREVER.

NINETY-ONE PERCENT of the women said they would give up sex with a man before they would give up his hugging and caressing. The women gave this question less thought than any other question. Their response was instantaneous, almost to the point of being automatic. As I listened, there seemed to be no doubt in their minds. If they had to choose, they would choose hugging and caressing over sex. Their comments were:

"No question about it ... I'd give up sex. Neither is appealing to give up, but between them, that's the way I'd go."

"I'd give up sex. I think that with some men, sex is sometimes a domination ploy with a winner and a loser, whereas hugging and caressing and holding hands and being close is a genuine, sharing kind of thing. Everybody wins in a hug."

"God, what a question. Forever?"

"Forever."

"So we're talking about what is more fulfilling. Well, I would not give up hugging and caressing." She laughed. "Sorry, sex. I'd give up sex. I think hugs are very important. At least three or four a day. You've got to hug your kids, and friends, and people you work with. I love touching, and I love people who touch me back."

"I'd give up sex in a New York minute. Hugging and caressing is important to me. When I come home from a tough day, if he hugs me, and holds me a minute, it reenergizes me ... and him too, if he'd just realize it. I get more from those hugs than being thrown down and laid. A *lot* more."

"I'd give up sex. I need the intimacy that comes with hugging and caressing."

The counselor said, "I'd give up sex. We can make monkeys nuts by not letting them be held or touched. It's pretty well been proven that we can live without sex, but we need touching for our well-being (Maslow, *Hierarchy of Needs*; Video: Salenger, Fred and Susan) Unfortunately, men have a lot of programming that says real sex is an orgasm. So, to the disappointment of women, they work as fast as they can to get the orgasm they want. Richard Pryor had a joke that said he didn't know anything about foreplay. 'One play, maybe two, and I don't want it to get away.' The difference is just letting yourself languish and love, and whatever happens, will. Sometimes it's no more than kissing and hugging, and sometimes it's intercourse. But it's important to our well-being that we immerse ourselves in each other, rather than connecting one dot to another ... so much time at dot one, then move on to dot two, etc. Most wives know when their husband is coming after them with sex in mind, by the way. From where he kisses her, she knows what dot is coming next. Dot connectors are missing a lot. There's much satisfaction to be gained for a man from hugging and caressing, too."

"I don't want to give up either, but if I have to make a choice, I'd give up sex. Sometimes maybe all I want is hugging and kissing, but he gets turned on and wants to get on with it. But I tell him, wait, wait, wait ... I want to be hugged and kissed plenty first."

"I'd give up sex. The nurturing I get (and him too) from hugging and caressing is very important. The reason I don't enjoy men who are a lot taller is that it's easier to hug a man nearer my size."

The widow of a construction company owner said, "I've had to give up both. But if you love someone it's okay, like when my husband went on the kidney machine. First I lost sex, then all of a sudden the hugging went away. So I lost both, and I didn't like either loss."

"Which did you dislike losing the most?"

"I could give up the sex easier. So that men understand, my husband's and my relationship progressed to another level that few people experience. We had more closeness and opened up to each other so much more when sex was out of the way. I probably won't marry again because I have experienced a high that few people know, and I won't be satisfied with less than that. Maybe sex was a problem for him and I didn't know about it ... it certainly was no problem for me. However, when sex was eliminated because of the kidney machine ... when we both knew it couldn't be and we no longer thought about it, that opened doors to another relationship that included more hugging. I'll never forget one day when we were getting ready to leave the country club where we golfed. He was going one direction in his car, and I was going another. We were smooching out behind the club house and the bag room guy caught us, and he thought that was so funny … here were these old people smooching, and he thought that was so cute and funny. For us, it was a moment we treasured the rest of his life. Keep in mind that my mother gave me a very healthy outlook on sex. I loved it and had a very fulfilling sex life. But if I had to choose one or the other, hard choice that it is, I'd keep the hugging and caressing, and just miss the sex."

The bank secretary said, "I'd give up sex. I'm reminded of just touching little fingers once in church. It's the tiny things that mean so much. There's nothing sweeter than to see a little old man and a little old woman having dinner when he reaches over and touches her, or she touches him. That's love."

"I'd give up sex. My first husband was a wham-bam artist. Hugs and caresses are absolutely essential to my well-being."

"I'd give up sex, because I need to be touched. With a lot of men, their sex business doesn't include much touching. But I need it."

Here are the views of two of the nine percent who would keep sex. "God, what a question. Let's see, there'd probably be a lot more sex if it was all only hugging and kissing. That would lead to sex. I don't know … fifty-fifty.

I was insistent. "You must make a choice."

"That's not fair. Where'd you get that question? Hopefully, with the sex, you could have both. I don't know."

"For the question to be revealing, you must make a choice," I repeated.

"Good grief. Well, if there's kissing, that for me means sex is coming. I don't want to give up sex, because if there's hugging and caressing, I'm a goner. If I have to make a choice, I guess I'd give up hugging and caressing and keep the sex."

Another woman said: "That is really an interesting question. I would rather have sex forever and give up the hugging and kissing. That is a new change for me. Not long ago my answer would have been the opposite. But at this moment I'm comparing affection versus passion. Okay, right now I want passion more than affection."

This last comment: "Tough choice. Because of the way your

question is worded, I'd give up sex. The reason is, if there's no hugging in sex, it's not the kind of sex I want involved with."

* * * * * *

When men meet someone new, I think many are nervous about how she may feel regarding previous women in their lives. So I asked:

What are your comments about other bed partners in your man's life: a) before you, and b) during his relationship with you?

THE WOMEN'S COMMENTS were:
"What happened in the past happened, but keep the details to yourself. Nothing will destroy me quicker than a man telling me that I'm good, *but* Suzie does such and so."

"Considering the threat of AIDS, and other STDs, it would make me uncomfortable if he had been involved with somebody in the past and hadn't been careful. I don't want a guy who has jumped into bed with anyone and everyone."

"If he isn't experienced with women, I don't want anything to do with him, because he may be living in a different sexual world."

"Women in his past don't upset me ... I've got him and they don't."

"Yesterdays are experience for tomorrows. I don't care who he has known, where he's been, or what he's done. All of his experiences helped shape him into the person I love today." She laughed and added, "If he's an especially good lover, I'd be grateful to them for teaching him."

"I wouldn't want a man who had no practice before I got him. I like a man who knows what he's doing. I thank those previous bed partners who were good teachers."

"I want him to maintain his contacts with former girls who were friends only. Former bed partners I want to be history."

"I would hope we could talk about past relationships, in hopes I could discover what went wrong ... why isn't he with her now? What happened? I would try to use the information to make our relationship better."

"His former bed partners were lucky girls."

How do you feel about other bed partners during his relationship with you?

IF THERE'S NO COMMITMENT, his bed partners are none of my business. However, if we're engaged, another bed partner would end it for me."

Other opinions were: "I used to be terrified at the thought of him sleeping with another. I used to think that if we women would just not get involved with another's man, it would end the problem. Now that I'm older, I see that men and women do what men and women do. Men are just as responsible as is the so-called other woman. Now I wouldn't hold her any more responsible than him. But it's still painful."

"I don't think there's a woman in the world who would accept another bed partner in her man's life. That would be degrading to me."

* * * * * *

A great fear of men's is that their woman may turn to someone else for sex. So I asked,

What could your husband do, or not do, that might cause you to consider a one-night stand, or even an affair?

THIRTY PERCENT said there was nothing their man could do to cause them to be unfaithful.

Examples:

"I'd get a divorce before I had an affair or one night stand."

"He couldn't make me have an affair. If he had one and I treated him in kind, that would just be two wrongs."

"He could do nothing to cause me to have a one night stand or an affair, because for me to do either would be hurting me."

"If he had an affair, why should I lower myself to his level? Somebody else, especially a woman I may not even know, is not going to determine how I act."

Twenty-one percent of the women had a "get even" mindset toward men who are unfaithful. One said, "If he were caught with another woman, I'd probably go out and do the very same thing."

Another said, "If he had an affair or one-nighter, I would get revenge. I'd find a man to screw as soon as I could."

The majority of women, forty-nine percent, said that what was more likely to drive them to someone else's bed was to be ignored, given no attention, or shut off sexually and/or emotionally.

"I could be driven to an affair if he ignores me, or treats me like I was there just to cook and clean and warm the bed."

"When I'm ignored for a long period of time, a real longing sets up. I'd take my sex to someone else if he ignored me for a long period of time."

"If he quit being caring, became unreceptive, and put up walls between us, I'd probably look to another for fulfillment."

"If he cut me off sexually long enough, and didn't give me any kind of physical contact like holding or cuddling ... not necessarily intercourse, I'd find somebody."

"If he wasn't interested in me ... my business, where I've been, where I'm going ... etc. Neglect me buddy, and you're going to pay for it."

* * * * * *

Is there a male who doesn't like to look at a female form? To find out how women feel about our looking at them, I asked,

How do you respond to a man, one who is unknown to you, ogling your body?

SEVENTY-EIGHT PERCENT of the women were turned off by ogling when they perceived it as blatant leering. They said:

"Depends on his attitude. If he's disrespectful, like he's mentally undressing me, I resent it. But in a respectful, intimate way, that's fine."

"Disgusting. I leave ... just walk away."

"Depends on how I feel about my body that day. If I'm secure with who I am and feel good about myself, I'll flirt back. But if I sense he's ogling my body for sexual purposes that my body could fulfill for him, I feel degraded and turned off."

"I may say something sarcastic to the guy, which usually goes over his head ... an indication of the limit of his brains."

"If it's obvious and blatant, I resent it. I'm not merchandise on the shelf."

"I get angry, and if he's obnoxious about it, I'll tell him to cut it out. Once I was on the executive floor delivering something, and the corporate attorney kept staring at my chest. I told him to cut it out. Later I heard he was saying I was rude to him. I wasn't rude to him ... he was rude to me, and his attitude makes me bristle."

"If they're looking at me with lust, I resent that. Look, but don't leer."

"I leave."

"I tell them to get their bug eyes off me."

"Makes me feel I was a thing, and that he's not seeing me as a person. He's an instant negative."

"No one wants to be leered at, unless she's a tramp."

"If he looks at me with a leer that says I'd like to stick it to you, he turns my stomach."

"I think he's a jerk."

"If he's just looking, that's fine. I just don't want him growling or whistling."

* * * * * *

How do you respond to a male that you are intimate with ogling your body?

EIGHTY-TWO PERCENT of the women said they liked to be ogled by a man they are intimate with. "Shows he's interested in me." "Flattering."

"A little embarrassed, but I like it."

"Ogled by my man? I love it."

"I like it, but if I'm a little overweight, it makes me uncomfortable."

"It makes me feel like I have a power there. Gives me a plus feeling."

"A proper amount of ogling my body is fine, but don't overdo it to the point of wearing out your welcome."

"After all, if I'm not pleasing him, I may as well not be with him."

"I ogle back."

"That's part of our intimacy. I love it."

"I didn't like my former husband ogling my body. If he couldn't talk to me, or listen to me, he may as well not ogle me. But for the man I'm with now, I love it."

"I want my man to ogle me."

"To be looked at by a man who is special to me is a compliment."

"Leering is for the bedroom, and then it's not a leer. It's more like a yum-yum."

* * * * * *

What are your feelings about a man who has Playboy/Penthouse/etc. AT THE TOP of his reading list?

THIS QUESTION IGNITED THE WOMEN into some of their longest answers. For instance: "He and I would have nothing in common. That kind of stuff doesn't blend with the type of man I want to be around. If that's his focus, what could I talk to him about that would be of value or interest to me? As far as I'm concerned, he wouldn't be enlightening conversation with any woman. His reading priority tells me he's more interested in my pants than my overall well-being."

Another woman said, "At the top of his reading list? Bless his heart, I feel sorry for him. The poor guy must be bored with life. There are so many other things that would be so much more enriching that could top his reading list. I don't mind if he reads it, but I do mind a lot if that's his number one choice. I don't consider those magazines as reading material. Lookee maybe. But reading? Ha ha."

"I'm a first amendment person. Everybody should be able to read whatever they want. My objection is with 'at the top of his reading.' He must be pretty shallow. I think he would not be much of a conversationalist ... I mean what could he talk about?"

"If that's his top reading, I would assume he is incapable of a fulfilling physical sex life with a *woman*."

"I don't think highly of that kind of man. Sometimes Jim will glance at one of those magazines, and so do I. But to the guy who has it at the top of his list? People I've known in that category tend to be insecure, dominating people. They strike me as mentally screwed up ... not knowing where they're going. They seem to hate women, by the way."

"Wrong kind of top priority reading, Joe. I consider such a man as numb, null, and void. He's a zero zombie in my book. He probably has no snap. Obviously he's not in the real world, because he can't deal with live humans, so he'd rather masturbate in the bathroom with his girlie magazine. He also probably sleeps with an inflatable doll. He's living in a dream world, unable to touch or reach out. That's scary. Talk about emptiness. To me, that type of man is in such fear and insecurity that I feel sorry for him."

"He's looking for a woman that exists only in his imagination, and I don't want to compete with an imagined image."

"I want a man who is interested in sex, but I don't want him to go overboard. Since I don't look like the girls in those magazine, I don't want him to start expecting that is what I'm supposed to look like. In other words, I don't want him off in some never-never-land, out of touch with reality. And for sure I don't want to risk him leaving me as soon as someone comes along with a body like what he sees in the photographs. His reading those magazines makes me uncomfortable."

"He's not a person I would be attracted to, because he would probably be one who thinks he's a great gift to women, thinks he's sexy, and probably has little depth and is not interested in cultural things versus sexy things. A shallow person."

"I think it's sad if those top his reading list. He's seeing only one dimension of a person … a flat view that has no depth. He's looking at sex alone. He's not looking at love, and love and sex aren't the same. Sex can be wonderful, but it's like icing on the cake. If you have a good sex life and a good relationship that includes intelligence, things in common, caring about each other, touching, WOW. But if it's just flat sex, it's not real. It's not full or rich."

"If that tops his reading, there goes the candlelight dinners. Get yourself and your magazine out of my life."

"Stupid. That's sex as a bodily function, like pissing and shitting. I doubt if that man knows how to love another human, let alone a woman. In bed he is mechanical, with no feeling for me and probably no deep feeling within himself. Just a surface shot. He doesn't know what he's missing."

"Oh God, there's no hope for such a man. I personally think bodies are wonderful, naked and unnaked. When *Playgirl* and *Viva* came out, I bought copies. But the publishers were surprised to discover they sold more magazines when naked men's bodies were in a picture sequence that implied a romance or fantasy relationship. Women were more turned on by those relationship themes than simply by some big dude with his thing hanging out. I think the pain for most women about their bodies is they don't have an accurate idea of how good their bodies look. Girlie magazines are not how women's bodies look. Those photos are airbrushed. When men lock onto those magazines, they have one box they fit women into. As soon as you don't fit the box, you get the heave ho, honey. You're history. These guys look to a woman to fit his image of a woman so people will think he's great, wonderful, and all that. He's more worried about his ego than he is about you. To him, you're a thing, and that's what I find sad."

"Guys who read those magazines aren't mental giants in my eyes."

"Every man I've known who bought those magazines said he bought them for the articles. That cracks me up. Who are they kidding?"

"Those magazines make it difficult, because us real women don't have the advantage of going through our day airbrushed."

"I have teenage sons, and I would be lacking as a mother if they got to be sixteen without knowing what a naked lady looked like. But to have those magazines at the top of their reading list is like seeing nothing but X movies and excluding some really good Hollywood stuff."

"I don't want the unfair competition. I believe in the real world of what's happening right now. I see no point in doing what ever they're doing to themselves to have to look at those magazines. I think those men are dissatisfied with what they have at home or are dating. I don't think satisfied men read those magazines."

"For me, sex is the sacrament of love. I hate those magazines because they cheapen that sacrament."

"I read them too. It basically says he enjoys the female body."

"His reading those magazines makes no difference to me."

"His interest in those magazines says he's not gay, that sex with a woman is okay."

One woman said she felt sorry for women involved with men who have these magazines *at the top* of their reading list. She smiled. "If her body, body parts, and face are less than pictured in a centerfold, he is likely to prefer intercourse in silence, in the dark, and/or with eyes closed to avoid looking at her. Under those conditions he can mentally eliminate you from the scene and blast his sperm into a fantasized centerfold … a whore could give him an identical outcome." She chuckled. "About all he'll remember about you is your phone number and address." She laughed. "And they expect *you* to have a centerfold body while many of them are flabby and have potbellies." She frowned. "Probably an equal number of women fantasize during sex in the same way." She became thoughtful a moment, looked me in the eye and added,

"I think women married to such men are tempted to be unfaithful more often than other women." She looked away. "And it's my observation that these types have little more to offer than raw, short-term, non-romantic sex." She looked back at me. "Often they are insensitive, in and out of bed. Almost always they are poor long-term lovers." She shrugged. "As far as I'm concerned, these guys are nothing more than another quick relationship, or serial sex fix that invariably ends in a woman feeling empty, frustrated, and depressed." She laughed again. "I'd rather use a vibrator than let one of these men touch me."

* * * * * *

The purpose of my next question,

Were you molested as a child, or raped at any time in your life?

was to give me an idea of how being molested as a child or raped as an adult may have biased their answers as to how they now interact with men, or how such events may have affected their individual lives. I got more than I bargained for. For one thing, I nearly fell off my chair the first time a woman said she was molested by her grandfather. When my research began in April of 1986, this was not a commonly known occurrence. Since that time, others have confirmed my findings. As it turned out, grandfathers, fathers, and stepfathers share the top billing as molesters among the one hundred women I interviewed. I was also startled at the percentage of women who had been molested or raped.

Forty-six percent of the women I interviewed said they had either been molested as children or raped as adults. This is a higher percentage than any survey I know of (per Biology 356, Human Sexuality, taught by Dr. Randy Thornhill, University of New Mexico). Keep in mind that nearly every rape survey contains the caveat that rapes are almost universally underreported. Adding to the confusion is the recent controversy over the new idea of "repressed memories." In defense of the results of my survey, it was done before repressed memory theories had surfaced.

Additionally, I can fathom no reason for the women I interviewed to lie to me.

Topping the list of molesters/rapists were:
Fathers   20%
Grandfathers   20%
Stepfathers   20%

The remaining forty percent of perpetrators consisted of brothers, uncles, preachers, family friends, and strangers. Some of their comments were:

"When I was ten, a friend of the family was an usher in a movie. During a movie he came next to me and was all over me with his hands and fingers, whispering lewd stuff in my ears. Shaking all over and scared to death, I got away and sat with friends. Well, he called my mother and told her I was causing a disruption in the show and to come and get me. She stomped in and jumped all over me. I hadn't said a word to my friends about what had happened, and of course was amazed to see my mother. I was upset from getting fondled and confused by my mom's giving me 'what for' ... which I considered was a double whammy. To this day I've never told her."

"When I was seven or eight, I was raped by my uncle, grandfather, stepfather, and dad. It affected me so much that on my honeymoon, I was terrified and wondered what I had gotten my self into. My husband was very understanding and patient. He told me not to worry, that I didn't have to have sex with him that night. It took a month for him to gain my confidence enough for me to get up the courage. I love him so much for that. He's a kind and gentle man I'd do anything for. It's thirty years later, and we have a beautiful sex life."

A four-foot-eleven, 103-pound woman occasionally takes her portable radio to the cemetery and dances on the grave of the grandfather who raped her when she was six.

There weren't many comments to the question of rape or molestation. Mostly the women simply answered "Yes" or "No," as if a raw nerve had been touched and they wanted to move on as quickly as possible. It was so difficult for one twenty-seven-year-old to talk about her being molested as a child, that I was the first person she had ever told. After talking with them, I have a better idea of how violated these women feel.

It is my observation that these women are more complicated. They also seemed less "happy" than women who had not been violated by a male. Generally, life seemed more difficult for them. Two that I know of have attempted suicide, and another considered it. Their divorce rate was a fraction over eighty percent, compared with fifty-four percent for women who hadn't been sexually violated. On the other hand, I found this group of women more interesting, even challenging. Remarkably, I didn't sense that they were rabid man-haters. Their defense seemed to be to restrict how far they allow individual men into their lives. In other areas of their lives these women also seemed extra cautious about extending trust.

* * * * * *

In light of current information on sexually transmitted diseases, my question,

What is your level of concern about herpes (0-10), AIDS (0-10), other STDs (0-10)?

now seems superfluous. Therefore, I'll dismiss it by pointing out that without exception each of the women were concerned. AIDS worries them most, rating a level of concern averaging 9.3 on a scale of one to ten. Herpes averaged 8.5, and other STDs averaged 8.3. The majority of their answers were short and to the point. The longest comments the women made on this subject were:

"I think the 60s and 70s were played pretty fast and loose. Today, if you're in a relationship and know he is screwing around with somebody else, and you're not using a condom, that's Russian roulette with a bullet in every chamber."

"I date a doctor and hear the horror stories. Ten on each."

"I have chosen to be celibate because of the threat of AIDS."

* * * * * *

At the time of your first sexual experience, for which reason did you choose to let it happen? a) romantic fulfillment, b) heat of passion, c) to deliberately lose virginity, d) curiosity, e) rape.

Forty-five percent said they succumbed to romantic fulfillment.

Nineteen percent admitted to heat of passion.
Nineteen percent gave curiosity as the reason.
Twelve percent were raped.
Five percent deliberately lost their virginity.

Comments were:
"I was in love with this boy, and we were about to move away. My mother forbade me to see him. I wanted that person to be the one to take my virginity. I had to beg him, because in those days guys didn't do it with nice girls, and I was a nice girl. I felt terrible, but he was my first love, and I wanted to give him my first love."

"Curiosity. I'd heard about it for years but never experienced it. So on that stupid day and at that stupid moment, I did it. It was a disaster. After it was over I was baffled as to why everybody seemed so ripped up over that deal."

"Peer pressure. All my friends had done it, so I thought it time." She laughed. "He thought it was because he was irresistible."

"I was fifteen. I knew nothing of romantic fulfillment until I was twenty."

"I was a virgin on my wedding night. That was my determination. I felt that was the greatest gift I could give him."

"We were both totally in love and both virgins."

"I lost my virginity on my wedding night. I dated him four years, and sex was something we chose not to do until we were married."

* * * * * *

The following are a few general comments offered by the one hundred women about sex:

T HE FORTY-ONE-YEAR-OLD CLIENT representative for a temporary help firm had this to say to "John Doe":

"When I was growing up, I was led to believe that intercourse would be a grand trip, with a toe-curling, starburst-and-fireworks climax. At first, it wasn't that way at all. Before my early thirties I thought maybe I wasn't all there. Then I discovered that I really was a sexually normal female. I found out through reading, and conversations with other women, that I had a clitoris. I found out that device is the main stimulation point for females ... our magic button. Most men don't know that. Why won't men pick up a book and find that out, or discuss it among themselves?"

I answered, "Probably because a man doesn't want to admit, especially to another male, that he doesn't already know all there is to know about sex." I shrugged. "Why aren't women more willing to teach a man?"

She laughed. "Maybe because we're afraid he'll show how smart he is to another woman." She turned serious. "Maybe we're the insecure ones. Anyway, I, and many of my friends, felt we weren't normal ... we felt we're supposed to orgasm just like he does, during normal intercourse. Many women still don't know better. They simply fake it and suffer in silence. Most of us don't automatically know what a powerful invention our clitoris is. I found out by researching ... reading, and talking with girl friends. But to approach my closest friend and say, 'I've got to talk to you about this clitoris thing' was one of the hardest things I ever did in my life. I had talked to my mother about it, and she was no help at all. Apparently she comes only from intercourse. My sister said she could come either way ... clitoral stimulation or intercourse. But I only come externally, via clitoral stimulation. So I wasn't getting anywhere by talking with my sister or my mother, but at least it was a start." She continued. "The way men are makes it difficult to tell them what we need in sex."

"Define 'how men are.'"

"Well ... you know ... pleasure through his penis is so direct ... so simple ... *wham-bam* ..." She laughed. "Women really aren't all that complicated ... but we are a shade more complex than *wham*."

Tentatively, I asked. "For those men who don't understand how a woman's sex area is constructed, would you mind drawing a mental picture for them?"

A big smile lit her face. "Start at a woman's tummy. Moving down, you come to her pubic hair ... then proceed on down, to the loop that forms the top of what men would consider to be a woman's opening. At that point, gently probe inside. Just below that loop is her clitoris." She took a breath. "Think of her clitoris simply as a miniature penis ... it even has a hood ... and its location corresponds to where the root of a male's penis originates from inside his body. Normally a clitoris lays limp under its hood ... until it is stimulated.

"When a woman becomes aroused, that tiny organ enlarges, becoming firm and erect with an elongated miniature shaft and head. Although almost hidden, a sensitive man with a soft touch will feel its presence. To give a woman an orgasm, that little penis must be stimulated by massaging. A finger or two works fine." She leaned forward. "Keep the clitoris and surrounding skin lubricated by juices from her vagina, which is well below her clitoris. She should signal to her partner by some method about when to increase or decrease pressure, and how fast or slow she wants to be rubbed ... preferably in a circular motion." She settled back. "So, we are a little more complex than a man, but not all that much for one who is willing to learn." She smiled. "If a woman is so inclined, she could be perfectly satisfied by a ninety-year-old man who knows what to do."

"Your description is a powerful revelation ... thanks for your frankness." I made a small salute. "That took courage."

She blushed and laughed. "I'm amazed at myself."

"Let me ask again ... why aren't more women willing to teach a man about the female body?"

She answered with a question. "Why aren't fathers willing to teach their sons? Aren't fathers the logical ones?" Her voice had a snap.

"Intelligent idea, but I have no answer. Besides, that could be a whole new book."

"Then I'll answer your question: why aren't women willing to teach a man about a woman's body?" She shrugged. "There's a barrier there that we're embarrassed to face, especially when he's hot to trot under the sheets." She took a breath. "Hey, we're talking about a delicate time and a fragile male ego." She chuckled. "I guess we're afraid that if we start talking too much at that moment, he might fold." She looked down. "To avoid embarrassment, the woman settles for less, or takes care of herself later." She looked back up. "But men don't help, because they seem not to want to hear. And a woman doesn't want the man to feel bad or inadequate, so when they make love, she acts like everything is fine. It's a Catch 22." She thought a moment. "At the same time I suppose it's unreasonable to expect a man to automatically 'know' her. Heck, the man I married at eighteen ... he was twenty-one ... never knew how to handle me ... I was rarely satisfied throughout our thirteen years together."

I asked, "Could it be you didn't pursue satisfaction because you depended on him to be the great sex expert and solve your problem?"

"Sure. And twenty-three years later I know that a lot of men act like they know, but when you get down to the wire, you discover they don't. So when I found out my first husband wasn't an expert, I wanted him to know what I needed so badly I could have killed him. But after a while I grew tired of telling him. And I was afraid that if I insisted, 'Look, this is how I am, and this is what I want,' I might hurt his feelings. I found out what *I* wanted only after years of timid brain-picking of girl friends. After I learned about myself and decided there was nothing wrong with me ... that I really was normal, I realized my needs could be communicated to a man sensitive enough to listen and smart enough to understand, in less than a minute. For that matter, all I had to do was show him ... demonstrate by letting him watch me." She smiled. "With my new husband, we have a real simple agreement: after I'm satisfied, he can do anything to me he wants." She sighed. "I had a girl cousin whose husband, after twenty years, found out she had been faking orgasm all that time. He was crushed. It tore him up so bad he wanted to get into group sex where they swap partners. But really it was her fault. For twenty years she cheated herself. The fake orgasm syndrome almost ruined their marriage. She hates herself for those lost years. But after all, she says, she was just trying not to make him feel bad. She almost ruined the whole deal. In the end he felt like an absolute retard." She smiled. "Men are surprised at what I tell them about female sexuality. My uncle was married twenty-three years and said as far as he knew, his wife had never come. I asked him why he supposed she hadn't; could it be that he didn't know how to handle her—didn't he give a damn about her needs and wants? In fairness, she was probably too shy to tell him what she wanted ... which makes it partly her fault. Then again, it seems to me something was basically wrong. Otherwise, why didn't she feel comfortable enough to talk to him about it? But twenty-three years? Give me a break. She was probably afraid of bruising his ego, and he was probably afraid of her. But how could he have been satisfied without being interested in her satisfaction? I have a hard time with that. He's missing such good sex ... he really doesn't know what it's about until he has a woman as satisfied as he is. Men talk about wanting to get hold of a tiger ... they talk about these 'tiger' women. Well, they've got a tiger in any woman if they just knew how to get 'em to react... be soft and sensitive enough to get her to respond. We know men are fragile, but we also know they are human. We want to see the human side of a man. Don't be afraid ... women are human, and understanding. The more sensitive a man is, the more we're going to love 'im. You're always for the underdog ... he's not going to look less of a man ... he's going to be loved to death."

"That's nice to know, but I think that deep down, many men envy a woman's ability to have multiple orgasms. And I think the thought of this capacity bruises some men's competitive gene."

"I'm not calling for multiple orgasms, which he can give me with his hands anyway." She stopped abruptly. "Competitive gene?" She giggled. "How funny." She giggled again. "Anyway, what I'm asking for is sensitivity to what gives me pleasure." She took a deep breath. "To be satisfied, a woman doesn't have to have multiple ejaculations from her man. If he has good hands and fingers and is aware that she has breasts, he can give her umpteen orgasms without ever unzipping his pants. Besides, if he cares about her ... that's the key word ... *if he cares about her* ... her excitement of the moment should excite him too, and he may be surprised to find himself recharged sooner than he thought possible." She paused. "That's the difference between a man and a boy ... the boy just wants to get his rocks off. The man wants that too, but along the way he'll also see to it that his woman is totally satisfied." She looked me in the eye. "And for heaven's sake, tell John Doe that a woman chooses to climax more than once, only *if she wants to*. Some days her hormones aren't aligned, or she simply isn't in the mood. Just because we're capable doesn't mean we want to 'perform' every time."

A thought came to me. "Is it possible that a reason women can have multiple orgasms is because they don't ejaculate? And do women appreciate the degree to which ejaculation temporarily drains a man?"

"Of course we do ... we don't expect multiple bolts from a man." She became pensive.

"With my first husband, sex was a one-time shot. With my second husband, we were in bed one day from nine o'clock in the morning to one-thirty that afternoon. But it was the touching, kissing, and holding ... that's what it was all about for me. Sure, more orgasms happened ... but for me, the holding and cuddling was the most important." She eyed me. "Don't misunderstand ... there are as many kissy-cuddly days as wild, passionate clays."

I looked her in the eye. "But for a man who isn't familiar with how a woman in constructed, the thought of hours in bed with a naked lady who wants sex is scary."

She leaned forward. "That's what we're talking about… if a man will take the time to learn about a woman's body, it won't be scary. He'll know that he can bring her to ecstasy by stimulating her clitoris with his fingers … knowing that she's satisfied ought to relieve a great deal of that scariness." She leaned back. "And let me tell you this … after a woman has had a clitoral orgasm, she will want his penis inside her. It's then that he'll pleasantly discover it's nine times easier for her to come again, vaginally, and often simultaneously with him. His bonus for being knowledgeable of how she functions is that after his fingers do their charm, she is going to do everything possible with, or to, him to make sure he is satisfied." She took a breath. "That's how great sex happens."

"You make a good case, but some men will remain skeptical."

"For heaven's sake, why?"

"Because they've heard locker room stories about bedroom marathons and aren't sure if it's true or just macho bragging. Either way, the rumor makes them uneasy and suspicious. They think the rumors are about an insatiable woman." I took a breath. "If you so much as hint that you'd like to stay in bed with such a man, it's easy for him to become afraid you are 'one of those,' and there goes his ego and confidence … on the spot. It terrifies him to think that he might not be able to handle you …"

She interrupted me with measured words. *"If he's terrified, it's because he hasn't taken the time to learn how to make love to a woman."*

"Okay, but these same men are also afraid that if they don't stay in bed with you, you'll dump 'em and look for a man who will."

She scoffed. "That's crazy. Satisfying my sex urges won't keep me from looking for another man."

Her answer startled me. I asked, "Would you tell John Doe what might cause a sexually satisfied woman to look for another man?"

"Sex is a bonus in a relationship, not its foundation. I could have all the sex in the world, but if my emotional needs aren't being met, we're in trouble."

"Emotional needs, such as?"

"Such as listening to me … listening to me talk about my problems, and at least empathizing with me." Her eyes blazed. "He doesn't have to fix it … in fact, don't even try. Just give me a safe shoulder to cry on without belittling me or putting me down. And please don't pick that time to tell me about his problems. The solution is, there is no solution. *I just want to be able to talk about it, not get advice on how to solve it.*" She softened. "All a woman wants is for someone to know, and recognize, when we are hurting." She glanced at me. "When I've got a man who cares enough to genuinely listen to me, if he's also good in bed, it's difficult for another guy to turn my head very far." She paused. "I don't understand why men don't get that ... it's so simple."

I laughed. "Sounds like what a lot of us men could use is six weeks of *Listening & Empathy Camp*."

She laughed and cocked her head. "Tell me ... what makes some men different from others in bed? Why do some men stay aroused longer? Or recharge quicker?"

"Because of you ... your receptiveness and willingness to continue to make love with him. That is a total turn on for a man. Convey, *very gently*, that you want more sex, and chances are, he'll stay with you as long as you want."

She glanced at me, and then away. "My second husband admitted that to me. He said he had never been like that with his first wife."

"I believe any healthy male is capable of a bedroom marathon," I ventured. "They just don't know because they have never been led, *gently, carefully* (lovingly), into the risk of finding out. I didn't know my full potential as a man until I was led into risking. I was surprised at myself. Oh, I was apprehensive. I was ready to get out of bed and go on about the day. But she held me back, and then led me gently, sweetly back into her sexual repertoire. To my surprise, she wasn't asking more than I could give. When 'our day in bed' began, I had no idea it would be a new (marvelous) experience. I didn't realize that until it ended hours later. Until then my sexual limits had been in my imagination. (Since then, one of my favorite sayings has become, 'Argue for your limitations, and they are yours.') She had a better understanding of my limits than I did. I think if a woman encourages a man, in a nonthreatening way, to stay in bed with her after ejaculation, both he and she will be surprised at how soon he may be recharged."

"Dan, recharge isn't the point." She seemed a little impatient, and her words were slow and paced. "I don't need a man to ejaculate into me for me to be satisfied. He can totally satisfy me with his finger." She leaned back. "The point is, I want him to lay in bed with me and to enjoy each other's closeness. At that point, I care more for his closeness than continued intercourse. Take time for a rubdown, or whatever. If he will just take time with her, things will probably happen again ... sooner than he thought possible, and on a whole new level." She paused. "For a woman, time like that with a man is so powerful that it creates an almost unbreakable bond."

"The key element is, she must lead him gently," I repeated. "At first he may be alarmed at not being sure of what he's getting into ... . He may even panic at the thought of being 'out of control.' If he becomes too afraid of the unknown, he'll probably fold. But if he has guts, and she is nonthreatening, he'll stay around, if for nothing more than out of curiosity."

"Then why won't more men risk that?... What have they got to lose?" she asked.

"Ego. That fragile male ego ... their very soul."

"Then please tell men they must understand that women like a softer man who is willing to show that he has some sensitivity for a woman's feelings. That's what a woman wants to see in a man."

A fifty-two-year-old bank teller said, "Please tell John Doe that if a man will just ask a woman what she wants, she'll be so appreciative to know he cares about her feelings, she'll want to satisfy him in ways he only dreamed of." She thought a moment. "For example, if she tells him that to have her breasts sucked feels good, and he follows through, she will probably be driven to reciprocate." She took a breath. "Now, tell the guys who believe they are satisfying a woman by delaying ejaculation until they *imagine* she has climaxed, they're wrong. Without clitoral stimulation first, it is difficult for a woman to come vaginally. When he just keeps on going and going, she begins to think she doesn't turn him on enough to satisfy him." She shrugged. "It is a downer that she simply may feel she has to endure ... or she fakes it, to end it." She arched an eyebrow at me. "It would be difficult for her to get by with faking an orgasm, if the man realizes how overly-sensitized a woman's clitoris is after a genuine orgasm."

"Would you mind explaining?"

She lowered her gaze modestly. "To continue to stimulate her after she has had a clitoral orgasm is akin to being tickled to the point where you can't stand it anymore." She hunched forward slightly and hugged her shoulders with crossed arms. "If you touch her there, an involuntary reflex will cause her to back away ... like jerking back from an electrical shock." She paused reflectively. "But, if she's faking it, touching her clitoris wouldn't cause her to jerk away." She took a long deep breath and let it out slowly before continuing. "And please give this advice to those men who *are* considerate enough to stimulate her clitorally: After her orgasm, give her time to come down from it. She needs time to recoup .... You wouldn't want someone to bang your penis with a hammer right after you came, would you?" She took a breath. "Generally, I would say it's okay to go ahead and slowly penetrate her. But before beginning *gradually* to do your thing, let her enjoy the fullness of touching and loving. I think she'll let you know when she's ready for more." She stopped for another deep breath. "On the other hand, if her partner skipped stimulating her clitoris, and their lovemaking results in a vaginal orgasm anyway, she's even more sensitive to clitoral stimulation. And during that wonderful relaxed feeling while both partners are coming down, the woman is still highly stimulated. In fact, if a man will take time to gently touch and stimulate her, often she can climax again, clitorally ... an added bonus to her sexual experience."

I was amazed and grateful for this woman's candor. After a brief silence that was a bit awkward for me, another delicate question formed in my mind. Wanting to get as many answers as I could, I asked, "Is there a difference for you between a clitoral or vaginal orgasm?"

She looked down again and thought a moment before replying. "For me, Dan, my clitoral orgasms seem to be more of an intense, spiky feeling ..." She held one hand up and squeezed it into a fist. "Focused, like that. On the other hand, vaginal orgasms seem rounder ... fuller." She shivered. "They exhilarate my whole body's energy." She smiled. "Then there's my 'G' spot orgasm. That one puts me in a different, *primal*, even scary dimension, as if I've been transported mentally to another universe. But to reach a 'G' spot orgasm, *and have my ejaculation*, my partner has to be incredibly special to me ... a man I trust enough to turn my psyche over to, because I'll be in no shape to be responsible—as if only my body were still here—as if I'm scared to death of being left out there as a mindless spirit, unable to get back into my body, and somebody needs to be paying attention, to bring me back to the planet, somebody I trust. *I've only had all of that with one lover.*" She sighed. "But, back to the guy who thinks he's satisfying a woman by just grinding away. Hopefully some kind woman will care enough about him to show him what she really wants." She sighed deeply, and her features relaxed into a broad, knowing smile. "However, when it all does fall into place and both are satisfied, all of that wonderful mutual pleasure blossoms, because one or the other was willing to reach out and risk." She sat up and folded her hands across her knees. "And isn't that what it's all about—satisfying each other's needs?" She smiled again. "Dan, I hope this helps men realize that although people often think women and men are from different planets, and we may be a little different sexually, our needs are about the same."

"I was thinking that." I was also pleasantly astounded by how much this woman was willing to divulge. "I appreciate how open you've been."

She smiled again. "Frankly, I am surprised at my frankness with you."

We laughed and she added, "I think that one or both of us is unequalled in polite audacity."

We laughed again before exchanging thanks and goodbyes.

Thinking I'd "heard it all," I was pleasantly surprised by equally revealing comments from a thirty-one-year-old supermarket checker I interviewed on her lunch hour. Sitting on green grass under trees shading the edge of a parking lot, she had this to say about sex: "There would be a lot more female happy campers if the John Does of this world would get over their *wham-bam* mentality." She tossed her head. "For a woman, and I think for sensitive men too, a sexual climax begins long before either of them get near the bedroom."

She paused while a strolling mother with a toddler in tow passed. "A starburst climax can have its origin early in their day together, with simple things, such as small talk while preparing and sharing a meal, or while sitting in warm sunlight sipping coffee and discussing how each other's day went—or talking about a current news story ... or what the kids have done.... You know, it doesn't have to be anything deeper than simply sharing life's small happenings."

She brought her knees up under her chin. "During their time together, little pats here and touches there get expressed between them ... pats and touches not meant to go anywhere at that particular moment—they will just happen as a natural flow." She glanced at me with a sly grin. "As inevitable as the tides, sexual tension will gradually rise." Pausing, she added in a softer voice, "At some point your interactions reach a crescendo." Her eyes focused on the distant mountains as she appeared to visualize an inner scenario. "Aroused and stimulated—and filled with increasing passions made hot by anticipations—in both your minds' eyes, you picture your bodies coming together.... You imagine waves of wonderful feelings washing over you ... feelings you know will soon culminate in an overwhelming warmth."

A jet from the airport climbed into the sky, its noise temporarily drowning out our conversation. When it had passed, she continued. "It's as if the two of you have been wafted upward on a magic carpet through the clouds, up onto a mountaintop ... and into total peace." She paused, as if remembering a particularly blissful experience. Then she leaned forward. "Once you both have climaxed, *the second half of the trip lies ahead.*" She glanced pointedly at me. "*A lot of men don't seem to understand this second part of making love to a woman!* Now, I'll tell you for sure, they don't know what they're missing ... so pay attention."

To say the least, I was all ears.

She took a deep breath. "I think most women hate it when a man jumps out of bed to go wash, right after their lovemaking." She paused and shook her head. "It's as if he thinks we've made him dirty ... or that he can't stand a woman's juices on his thing. Some of us take that as an insult." She looked me right in the eye. "Would you please tell men not to be in such a hurry.... Tell them to spend time with her ... savor *with her* the journey of coming down from the mountaintop, hand-in-hand, blanketed in a warm glow. Truly, those moments can be just as beautiful and just as rewarding as the trip up."

She sighed and was quiet a moment. "Besides, taking the time to bask in the afterglow with her, as she returns to reality, completes the cycle.... It's an important part of the full enjoyment of sex. It will also make her feel that you care about her ... that she's cherished. And isn't that another part of what sexual satisfaction is about? But remember—" She gestured with her thumb backward over her shoulder. "The whole journey started back there, at some place in an ordinary day's routine." Her eyes softened and sought the mountains again. "And a complete journey sure beats *wham-bam.*" She glanced at her watch. "I hate to break this up, Dan, but I'm due back at work."

As we walked toward the supermarket's entrance, I turned to her in appreciation. "You've been extraordinarily straightforward."

She laughed. "I just want to see it when it's finished."

"I'll bring a copy ... you've earned it." We laughed again.

As you can see, these conversations are pretty good proof that a woman will talk with a man about anything. And these women convinced me that their needs, both sexually and emotionally, are not all that different from mine.

After listening to 100 women share their views on sex, I have this observation: It appears that women are capable of an almost unlimited spectrum of sexual joy. I liken female sexuality to the range and versatility of music that can be drawn from a fine violin. By contrast, from my male viewpoint, it seems that males tend to have the sexual repertoire of a one-note car horn. Maybe we men could learn some new and different harmonies from women that would mutually increase our sexual pleasures.

4

Women's Psyche about Men
A Look into that Part of Women's Minds that Deals with Men on Various Subjects

FEAR OF REJECTION commonly grips us males when we see a woman we want to know. So I asked,

What advice would you give a man who wants to get acquainted with you?

"TALK TO ME" is the most common answer I heard.
Examples included:
"I like the direct approach. Come up and introduce yourself and ask my name. Start a conversation. From there we may proceed. None of this 'Hey lady, wanna fuck?' garbage."

"Don't come at me with lines like, 'You look like someone I saw before.' Or, 'Don't I know your mother?' I'm turned off before you even had a chance. But, if you have something to say to me, say it. If you strike me as sincere and honest, I won't reject you out of hand. Tell me you're interested in me, but don't follow me. Communication is important ... take the risk. You might be surprised."

"If I were a tourist it would be easier to meet me. Just walk up and comment on the place we are visiting. No personal remarks. Just be friendly."

"Cruise over to my grocery cart and ask if I can hand you something that my cart is blocking. I'll say yes, and we'll have a conversation going. I don't want him to rush from the other side of the aisle and gush, 'Oh my God, I want to meet you ... WOW ... I've always wanted to meet a girl like you ...' and on and on. That's not conversation, that's bullshit. I would prefer the man to make the first move, to prevent anyone from getting the idea I'm chasing them. But if I want to meet him badly enough, I'll start a conversation."

"Sit down and visit with me. Get to know me, and don't be bashful about it. Talk to me."

"Don't ask me to a nighttime dinner and movie right off the bat. Invite me to a daytime movie, or an afternoon at the zoo. Give me some safe time to decide if I want to go out with you at night. Probably I will, but give me time to know you first."

"Too shy is better than too forward. If he starts a conversation with me, that tells me he's interested. If we're standing there reading a movie poster, he could ask me what I thought of the movie ... start the conversation."

"Don't try to please me. I want a man to be himself."

"Come to where I work rather than walking up to me in the store. Don't do that to me ... I'll leave the store. Come to my turf. I'll be gracious."

"Just walk up and introduce yourself. From the conversation that will follow, I can make up my mind about you."

"Don't give me that 'hey baby' stuff. Conversation is the way to open my door. And don't make snap decisions as to what I'm like. Get the facts by talking to me."

"Don't try to get me in bed on the pretext of 'getting to know me better.' Some flirting is okay, but be natural. Just say you'd like to get to know me better. That gets me right there."

"Don't make the first date a shower and dress affair. Make the first time coffee or Coke, preferably when we get off work. I like that because we can see each other more naturally, as opposed to all dressed up with best feet forward."

"Just talk to me. It's okay to compliment me on my dress or looks, as long as it's genuine."

"Don't give me a line. Be honest. To ask if I'm married or otherwise involved is okay. But don't ask me to bed before you even know me."

"One guy met me in a wonderful way. He sent a rose and didn't sign the card. It said, 'To somebody I'd really like to get to know.' Then one day he came to my desk with a rose like the one he sent. It knew it was him, and it was such a nice way to meet him."

"Get my eye and smile, but don't leer. Just tell me you think I look interesting, and you'd like to get to know me better. In other words, go for it."

"Goodness, talk to us like a person. Not like a man to a woman, but like a person to a person … as one human being to another."

"For him to say I'm 'interesting' turns a lot of doors for me. It means he thinks I'm intelligent and may have something to offer."

"Communicate. So many times people are hung up on this 'round the mulberry bush' crap. That's a stupid, time-consuming game, and it wastes valuable time. I can usually tell within a short time if there's going to be a possibility for a relationship. If there's not, I accept that fact, figure out what part of a relationship I might like to pursue with him, if any, and forget about the rest."

"Don't come on too fast. Let me know that you are attracted to me and like me and want to know me better, but don't rush."

"Come across low-keyed. Don't try to impress me. Just be yourself. Start a conversation in an honest, genuine way … not contrived. Focus on an interest we both may have, but don't make something up."

"If I glance at you and you glance back, just walk up and talk to me. If you smile, and I smile, I don't mind you coming and talking to me. Remember this rule: when a women smiles at someone, it generally signals she wants to meet them."

"Let's say you want to jump my bones. Baby, you gotta take it one step at a time. Sex isn't going to come right away. So if you want to meet me, talk to me."

"I think so many encounters with potential for a relationships are doomed from the start because we get from "A" to "B" too fast, without going through "C." By "A" to "B" I mean introduction to bed. Don't be in such a rush."

"Be honest. I mean, some men think they have to say something clever, which often comes off as ignorant. If he's honest, and we can tell in a second, it makes it easier to know if we'd like to know them better."

* * * * * *

Once we've risked meeting a woman, we don't want to inadvertently turn her off. Therefore, I asked:

What are turn-offs when you first meet a man and are making up your mind about him?

THEIR ANSWERS WERE:

"Coming on to me almost as soon as we've met. Flirting fast and so obviously that I'm sure you operate with every woman the same way you're treating me. Big turn off."

"Looking me over almost before you even know I have eyes. It's a real turn-off when you get to my eyes last. That attitude says you're the hunter, and I'm the prey. My attitude is run along, sonny boy."

"Turn-offs for me are bad body odor ... unclean hands ... unshaven."

"Talking about his job as if that's all he knows says he has no versatility at all. Either that, or he doesn't care anything about me or how I feel. Either way, he won't get anywhere with me."

"If he doesn't like himself, I'm turned off, because I probably won't like him either."

"Poor vocabulary, cursing, a lot of T talk."

"If we're in a public place, and he's talking to me while looking at other women, I'll dismiss him as soon as possible."

"No Mr. Macho act, please."

"Bragging about how much he makes, or inviting me to see his Porsche turns me off "

"I'm not turned off by his looks if he can talk intelligently."

"Smoking. Bragging. Sexual innuendos. Example: A guy told me not to judge him by the size of his hands. I asked what he was talking about and he said that the size of a man's hands wasn't related to the size of his penis. I told him I wasn't interested in proof and excused myself out of his life."

"If he acts like he's really hot stuff turns me off."

"Jeans so tight that his genitals strain against containment. Open shirts down to his navel are ridiculous and offensive."

"Those stupid lines, like 'you have the prettiest eyes,' etc. turns me off real fast."

"If I detect hostility in him ... I'm outta there."

"When I first meet a man, I take the role of the listener. But if I have to listen ninety-five percent of the time while he talks about himself, I'm turned off. Let *me* find out about you ... don't you tell me."

"If I sense that he wants to use me to fill space in his life for something he doesn't want to deal with, I'm turned off. Or, if he spouts big plans that are 'way down the road' in an attempt to get me into bed is a turn-off."

"Making remarks about women in his past. I don't like gossip."

"A proposition is a turn-off."

"If he can't sit still or repeats himself a lot, there has to be something wrong."

"I hate it when men ask my astrological sign. That's so ignorant, I mean, who cares? I just tell them my sign is STOP, and move on."

*　　*　　*　　*　　*　　*

Does any special physical trait turn you on when you meet a man or see a man in the store, parking lot, office, or on a movie/TV screen? In other words, do you have a fixed idea of how the "ideal" man should look?

I CONSIDER THIS ONE of three key questions in estimating the chance of a successful relationship. (See pages 175 and 183 for other key questions). The problem the above question addresses is the reality of a woman ever finding an earth-bound man exactly matching an imagined picture of what her ideal man should look like. Chances of her connecting a perfect mental match with a live male is next to impossible in one lifetime. The man she finally settles on may be close to her image, but he will always be an imperfect fit. The danger is that sooner or later she may pull away because of his "imperfections." Or, another guy may enter her sphere who comes nearer to matching her imagined profile, and number one will become history. On the other hand, a woman with a less rigid attitude about the physical makeup of the man she eventually chooses is more likely to be contented throughout her life.

Fifty-seven percent of the women said they appraised a man on his overall physique and appearance. Twenty-three percent said they looked first at a man's eyes, while eight percent checked his buns first. Five percent looked for what he might be like by studying his hands; four percent were impressed by his hair, and three percent by his smile.

The bank executive secretary said, "I don't look at just one thing. It's an overall package. His walk, the way he dresses. His features are important, but not the main thing. The way he moves, the way he feels about himself, the way he carries himself, is what I size up. I'm talking about first impressions. I'll get to the inner thing later. The inner man is the most important and will either make me run or stay."

The president of a personnel pool said, "I'm attracted to his physique. I want a guy who has a trim build. From there I go to facial features, and then personality. Personality is the most important. Even though I may be initially attracted by physical makeup, if there's no substance ... no personality, I'm gone. The man I have isn't physically attractive, but he has depth. He is warm and loving and has beliefs and takes stands in life. A guy like that is the top of the world to me."

The forty-one-year-old accountant said, "I'm not hooked by good looks, because personality is so much more important. Oh, a tall and good looking guy catches my eye. But if he turns out to be shallow, that ends it for me."

The TV news photographer said, "His eyes get my attention first. In his eyes, I detect either insecurity or security, confidence or lack of confidence, fear, anger. His eyes are really a window to his soul for me. I can also see the positive ones, like happiness, kindness, etc. But on a superficial level, I like butts. Men's asses look great. But his butt doesn't motivate me to pursue him. He's got to have a good head and a good attitude. In other words, it takes more than a couple of cute body parts to get me going. And massive muscles turn me off. They can hurt me. Besides, those types are so into themselves that they have nothing left for me. A small man comes on as less threatening."

The client service rep for a temporary help firm said, "I'm attracted to kind eyes. Eyes that don't say 'Check me out, Babe, I'm great.' I like a man's eyes that are taking in the world, rather than making a statement. I also like broad shoulders and thin hips. But if it turns out he has no substance, good-bye."

A forty-five-year-old teacher said, "Through a man's eyes I can measure his intelligence, humor, his admiration or lack thereof for me, his sexiness. Eyes tell me more about him than any other part of his body. My grandmother said eyes are windows to our soul, and I believe it."

A forty-one-year-old secretary said, "The first thing I notice are hands. They clue me as to what kind of work he does. His rings tell me his marital status. The way he picks things up or handles things tells me his level of gentleness. I can also detect if he smokes or not. And if he talks with his hands, that tells me he is an emotional man. If he is wearing jewelry I like, that's a clue that our tastes are similar."

Other comments were:

"If he has a nice body and a firm butt, he'll get my attention."

"If he doesn't look me in the eye, that makes me uneasy."

"I notice tight little buns ... a cute ass."

"I want him rugged, and not too perfect. When I see a man who is GQ perfect, it makes me think his values are more in looks than actions, and that he's too concerned with himself to have room for me. Mr. Perfect GQ tends to be more style than substance."

The twenty-seven-year-old retail clerk said, "I don't have a fixed idea of what my man should look like. If I did, I'd be in trouble, because the odds are so low that any man will ever perfectly match an imagined image."

* * * * * *

What could a man expect from you that you would dislike more than anything else?

THIRTY-THREE PERCENT answered to the effect of, "For him to expect me to be his servant." Thirty percent answered along the lines of, "I would dislike it if he tried to change me into something I'm not." Twenty-one percent listed sex on demand as their major dislike, including demands for sexual acts inconsistent with their values.

The TV news photographer said, "I dislike being expected to handle his personal business. For instance, I was engaged to a man when I discovered he had simultaneously asked four or five others to marry him. Well, they were calling, and he asked me to 'take care of that situation.' On top of that, I discovered I was laundering one of the others' panties who had popped out of his life just before I popped in. He was real upset when I told him I wasn't his social secretary/servant and he could go to hell."

The thirty-three-year-old airline pilot said, "I would dislike for him to expect me to do everything for him, such as pay his bills and wash his clothes when we're unmarried. Or expect me to always be there when he wants me to be. I work out of a schedule book, and I'd dislike for him to expect me to break my schedule for him."

The forty-three-year-old retail sales clerk said, "I would dislike being expected to answer at his beck and call. That includes sex, food, etc. The commando type. I'm not on earth to meet his needs. I'm here to share. It's not my job to make him happy. If I can help, I want to. But I won't be his servant."

One of the marriage counselors said, "I would dislike his expecting me to take care of him all of the time. On the other hand, when you're in a loving relationship, each will do a lot of things for the other. But when the expecting becomes a burden, and one or the other feel exhausted from being used, trouble is ahead."

The forty-four-year-old English teacher said she would dislike for him "to expect me to be something I'm not, such as no more than a show piece on his arm. Hey, once in a while that's okay, and even good for me. But don't make me only that to you."

One woman offered: "For him to try to mold me is a screaming message that says he doesn't find me attractive, loved, desired, wanted, and appreciated the way I am. If he wants to change me, obviously he doesn't like me. That scares the hell out of me."

The forty-one-year-old diagnostic technician said, "For him to expect me to be something I'm not is chewing at my core being."

The TV anchor person said, "I would not like sexual demands that I won't do, or housekeeper demands that are beyond reason."

The bank secretary said, "Don't expect sex on demand. If you want a night you'll never forget, I'll give it to you on *our* terms, but not on demand."

The forty-four-year-old radio salesperson said, "I would hate it if he expected me to answer to him, or ask his permission for every little thing, or account to him for every minute of my day. I'll call if my plans change, but I refuse to call out of fear. And I don't want to pick up after him, or be dishonest for him, such as lying or covering for him. All those are high on my dislike list."

Other comments were:

"I dislike being made to feel like I'm a machine ... a blow up doll for his pleasure ... his private whore."

"Don't expect me to do your laundry and have meals ready *every* day. And don't expect me to compromise my morals, because you'll lose that battle every time."

"Don't ask me to participate in kinky sex."

"Don't expect me to be cute and sexy 24/7/365."

"I hate it when a man tries to pin down every minute of my day. When I come back from the store, if he says, 'Oh, are you just getting back?' I hate the suggestion behind his remark."

"If I love him, there is nothing I wouldn't do that he asked of me. When I'm in love, I'll bend a lot."

"I would dislike for him to expect that I be somebody I'm not. But many men have been conditioned to that premise."

"How so?" I asked.

"Many times, when a woman finds a man interesting, she bends herself toward being what he wants her to be. Sometimes she is so eager she almost says, 'Give me ten minutes and I'll be whatever you want me to be, Sir.' When a woman compromises like that, she buries who she really is. That's fine for the nurturers and givers out there who are happy with that. But it's big trouble for those of us who insist on not being simply wired in as an extension of a man at the expense of being ourselves."

The wife who described herself as a "domestic Goddess" said, "I'm a nurturer. He could ask me for just about anything. No problem."

"Is there a point where you'd draw the line?" I wondered.

"Yes. I would dislike him expecting me to support him financially. And it took two relationships that foundered on those reefs for me to arrive at that." She laughed. "See, John Doe, you've got it made, and just don't know it."

* * * * * *

What could a man do, unexpectedly, that would please or pleasantly surprise you?

FORTY-SIX PERCENT said getting flowers, from a large bouquet to a single blossom, even including something wild picked along the way would please them.

Other preferences were:

"Drop by and grab me and tell me about a wonderful place he wants to take me, right now."

"To share a discovery with me tells me he thinks I'm above average in his life."

"After we've strolled the mall where I noticed a book I wanted, his personally bringing me that book later would please me very much. What thrills me is the fact that he notices what I like, and remembers. Remembering is what I love him for, far more than the gift."

"Once I came back from being out of town. The children were home with my husband. When I walked in, the house was spic and span. I was thrilled."

"Do things I don't like to do ... fill my car, wash it, clean up the house when I'm gone. Those are nice surprises, and it tells me I'm special to him."

"Be spontaneous. Decide on the spur of the moment to take us out to dinner, or call and ask me to meet him on the golf course. Spring something on me that we don't often do."

"Bring me a flower he picked, or anything that says he was thinking of me."

"Out of the blue, come home with tickets to a special show, or airline tickets to somewhere ... just him and me."

"An odd flower, like a dandelion in a vase with baby's breath. A personal note in the cereal box. May I make a speech?"

"Absolutely," I nodded.

"During courtship, these little surprises are common. After marriage, they tend to fade, and that's a shame. That element of flirtation should be kept alive throughout marriage. The marriages I see that work are like when she tells me her husband was flirting with her before they left for work. They keep that element of mischief that involves little things. But those little things carry big messages, such as 'I care about you; you're just as neat as when I first met you; I think of you often'; etc. And it's important not to expect anything in return. Too often we give a hug, or a kiss, or a gift, or sex in order to receive something in return. It's more pleasing and exciting if you do little things not as a trade, but simply because you want to. I think that element is too often too thin in relationships. One pleasant surprise I recall is receiving an old book from a guy who knew I liked old books. There was a note saying he thought I'd enjoy that book. I'm sure he expected nothing in return, other than his joy of sending it. That said he cared about me."

"I'd love it if he came home with wine and cooked a romantic candlelight dinner. It would be nice to be waited on, and for him to take charge of what is generally considered my responsibility. That would make me feel really special."

"Gifts make me uncomfortable, because there might be strings attached. I have a feeling that when a man spends money on me he expects something in return. I taught my children to be giving without thoughts of a trade. A guy asked me to go skiing. I told him I'd buy half of the gas and my own lift ticket, and that I wasn't spending the night with him. He said, 'Okay.' I liked that a lot."

"Send the kids to bed fifteen minutes early and not try to make love, but just hold me."

"Some surprise that is unstructured, like not on my birthday. Any unexpected show of affection. A single flower, even a dandelion out of the yard. The thought is what it's all about."

"Pop over with a bottle of champagne and tell me to dress up, we're going out."

"A surprise picnic lunch at some pretty place, like a quiet spot on a lake, or in the mountains. He took me once to a point on a lake, and I kept pinching myself, saying my God, this is stuff you see in the movies. I loved it."

"I wish he would surprise me by saying, 'Marry me.'"

* * * * * *

Who hasn't heard of divorced friends remarking, "We drifted apart," or "We grew in different directions." To address that I asked:

How important is it that you and your mate have similar interests, or even like vocations?

THE AD AGENCY OWNER said, "Some common interests are important. I play tennis, he doesn't; he likes to fish, I don't; I read, he doesn't. We share a house, yet I'm lonesome a lot of the time, and I'm stuck with it. Life could be better, if we shared more. What's that old saying? ... a joy shared is a joy doubled?" She looked thoughtful a moment, and shrugged.

A twenty-nine-year-old paralegal said, "I think similar interests boost a relationship. It opens up things to talk about besides the children, what color to paint the bedroom, etc. It gives them another area to share. That doesn't mean they couldn't have separate areas of their lives. They shouldn't necessarily be in lock step, but there should be some common footprints. As for like vocations, I wouldn't want competition from my husband."

The radio sales manager said, "To have a partnership filled with harmony and joy, you have to be able to play together. It's hard to play with someone who isn't playing on the same field as you."

The twenty-eight-year-old manicurist pointed out, "If you like opera, and he likes heavy metal rock concerts, you're in trouble."

The television anchorwoman said, "Similar interests are important to a relationship. For example, sitting in the middle of winter waiting to kill a bunch of animals isn't my idea of fun. But if I stay home by the fire, that's time we lost for being together, and that's a shame. Or, if he golfs and I shop, after a while we're going to grow apart. I think for a successful, long term relationship, you and your partner need to have one or more similar interests and goals. Think about it; it's pretty hard to keep in touch if you both are going different directions all the time. As for like vocations, we'd be competing, and that could cause friction."

A thirty-seven-year-old manager believes, "If you're going to be a team and hang out together, it's important that you have some like interests ... something that both like, that will draw you into the middle. The other way of that is, if I like Beethoven and he likes jazz, who are we going to enjoy hearing together? Like interests would be a part of the weave of a relationship. It can't be one hundred percent of it, but it is important to the whole of the fabric. I don't like the idea of like vocations ... too much chance for friction there."

The twenty-nine-year-old flight instructor and wife of an airline pilot said, "In our marriage, like interests have proven to be important. For instance, if I weren't in aviation, I'm not sure I could live with my husband if I didn't understand why sometimes he is frustrated at the end of some of his runs. The fact that I fly allows me to appreciate his job stress, especially on a really bad weather flight. If I weren't a pilot, I might not understand what it is like to command an aircraft full of people. I might not be patient with his frustrations when he comes home."

A thirty-four-year-old parts manager for a utility company said, "I was taught that the woman should learn to do what the man likes to do. So I learned to fish and hunt. But he was never willing to do anything I wanted to do. Over the years it has become a sore spot. If we had liked the same things in the beginning, I wouldn't have had to learn, and he wouldn't have to change ... we'd have been on the same track, instead of pulling in opposite directions. I'm not sure we're going to make it, and a lot of the reason is having so few common interests. In that kind of a mess, sex eventually becomes unimportant. At least it has for me. And when the kids are gone, all we'll have left is to sit and twiddle our thumbs. Common interests are a must if we expect to keep rolling along hand in hand."

* * * * * *

What kind of relationship would you prefer your man have with his a) mother, b) sisters, c) daughters, d) ex-wife?

OVERWHELMINGLY, the women wanted their man to have a good relationship with his mother, but they didn't want him to be a mamma's boy. Typical comments were:

"I want a man who loves and respects his mother because how he treats her is about how I can expect him to treat me."

"Men who have good relationships with their mothers are usually more sensitive."

"Men who are close to their mothers seem more educated about women. They seem to understand more about what a woman wants. I want a man who is close to his mother."

"Mothers, daughters, and sisters enrich my husband's life. The more his life is enriched, the more he has to contribute to mine."

"I want them in his life, but their mother's apron strings must be cut. I want to be his number one."

"His mother is dead, which was the biggest help to him that ever happened. She was very domineering ... tried to run both our lives. It's tacky for me to say it, but her death improved my life."

"I want him to be close to his mother, but not so much that I'm compared with her."

"The way he treats his mother is a clue as to what kind of person he is. How they interact is probably a clue as to how he and I are going to interact."

"I want a man to love his mother, because that helps him love his wife. But I don't want a mamma's boy."

"I take other women who are his relatives as my own."

"Praise God there are those other women in his life."

This reaction was common among the women as far as their man's relationship with sisters and daughters. The majority of women wanted those to be good, "because those people can teach him so much about women." However, there were wide-ranging views about his relationship with ex-wives. Comments were:

"For him to have a good relationship with his ex-wife is less stressful for me than a cat-fighting relationship with her."

"If he can get along with his ex-wife, fine. If he can't, I want her out of our lives."

"When she pisses him off, he's harder for me to live with."

"If they aren't constantly fighting, I prefer he have a working relationship with her."

"If there weren't children, it would be great if he cut her out of his life forever."

"I prefer he have a polite, civil relationship with his ex-wife. Not so much that he lunches with her, but not a hate relationship."

"I wish he had a wonderful relationship with her. Currently they are enemies, which is destructive ... awful. It affects my life negatively ... which she may know and is doing on purpose. That hurts everybody, including her children."

"I think these women are important in my man's life ... unless they are bitchy."

"Define bitchy," I asked.

"Possessive equals bitchy."

Random comments were:

"That he gets along with all of those people is a mark of maturity. His old girlfriends add to my life. And I'd like some of my old boyfriends to be mutual friends with my husband. But I think men have a harder time with that."

"I don't like it when he calls his ex-wife a bitch every other time he talks about her. He should have more respect for her, especially if she is the mother of his children. Out of respect as the mother of his children, he should at least pretend he likes her."

"If he needs to talk to his ex-wife every day, it makes me wonder why they got divorced."

"I wish his mother had raised him to take care of himself more than mamma doing everything for him. When we first married, he thought I should do more like his mother. I informed him I wasn't his mother and never would be."

* * * * * *

From previous questions, we have learned that often men and women innately have different priorities. To discover if there was a difference in how men and women think on yet another issue, I asked,

In what order do you think men want the following from women?
   a) housekeeper/cook
   b) sex
   c) companionship

FIFTY-SEVEN PERCENT of the women felt that *men's priorities* of wants from women were:
   sex
   housekeeper/cook
   companionship

I reversed the question and asked,

In what order would you prefer?

NINETY-TWO PERCENT of the women said their priorities were:
   companionship
   sex
   housekeeper/cook

A thirty-six-year-old housekeeper said, "I used to say men wanted sex as number one. But I'm finding that more and more men want a mate who is their best friend. Men are learning to value a woman they trust enough to unload on without being hurt. I think more and more men want companionship first and sex second.

The Alabama school teacher said, "I think some men look for real easy companionship. These guys look for women who aren't as smart as they are. They seem to want women who are really easy to be with ... real forgiving and nurturing and sweet. I wish they would choose more challenging companionship."

The motel night clerk said, "Sex is important to a man because his competitive world is tough. His sexual ability is one place he ought to be able to prove to himself he is a champion." She smiled and added, "But just remember ... in bed, a man is only as good as the woman he's with."

The camera repair technician believes that "men marry women as a matter of simple logistics. He gets TV dinners, pussy, laundry, etc., all under one roof. This saves him wasting energy in pursuing his needs individually. That conserves his energy for fighting the battles of life for him and *me*. It's totally logical."

Dr. John Gottman claims in *Why Marriages Succeed or Fail* (Simon & Schuster, 1944), that he found a correlation between the amount of housework a man did and his health ... that men who did more housework were healthier at the end of four years than men who did less. He believes part of the reason may be that resolving this domestic issue results in less conflict at home, and therefore less stress. Gottman also found that men who are involved in housework and childcare have better sex lives and happier marriages than men who do little or no housework and/or childcare. And Yale's Kyle Pruett says a ten-year study shows that a father's involvement in their child's first six months contributes to higher scores later on tests for motor skills and intellect.

* * * * * *

Many men take pride in their ability to "fix things." To find out how women rate that skill, I asked,

On a scale of zero to ten, how important is it that your man have handyman skills?

TWENTY-NINE PERCENT of the women rated those skills as either nine or ten in importance. The average importance given on a scale of zero to ten was 6.3. Their comments were:

"I would rather call a professional to do the job. I rate it four."
"Not important if you're rich."

"I rate handyman skills a ten, but it would not be a factor in determining a relationship."

"Ten for me, because it shows that a man is thrifty, not lazy, and if he can stay with a project to its successful conclusion, that shows he has the patience to keep working at something until he gets it right."

"I think it's important that one or the other know how to fix things. In my marriage, I'm the one handy person."

"A man who is handy at making broken things work turns me on. I'm just ah-h-h-h."

"It's a big help. I don't want to run around to have my car fixed."

"I don't expect him to be a jack of all trades. I can love an artistic person with few handyman skills."

"Zero with the plumbing, but ten for my car."

"After watching my dad, I thought all men had a fix-it gene. That is until my first husband embedded his shaver in a wall when it wouldn't work after he fixed it. I rate it at least a seven."

"If a man is not handy, he shouldn't complain about repair bills."

"I like a man who is handy, the same way I think a man feels about a woman who can cook. I have to be able to cook and he has to be able to fix things. That's how we survive. If it's a relationship, we have to take care of each other."

* * * * * *

Few people will argue with the importance of including a question about sense of humor in my survey:

How important is a sense of humor, on a scale of zero to ten?

SEVENTY-THREE PERCENT rated the importance of a man's sense of humor as a ten.

Thirteen percent rated its importance at a nine.

Eight percent rated your ability to enjoy a laugh at an eight.

Six percent rated a man's sense of humor at a seven or less.

Typical comments were:

"I rate it a ten. That doesn't mean he has to be Eddie Murphy or Robin Williams. He's just got to be able to laugh at the funny things that come along."

"Nine. And I don't mean joke humor. I mean a sense of humor about life in general."

"Ten. I love a guy who can make me laugh."

"My favorite men are those who can laugh at themselves. That shows they have a tremendous amount of security."

"Men who don't have a sense of humor aren't worth spending much time with. Life is too difficult not to be able to laugh at it when a situation needs a little humor."

"The ability to chuckle at yourself is a lot better than crying about some little problem that really is laughable, if you'll just sit back and see the human side. Humor gets me through lots of days."

"It's hard to be mad when you're laughing."

"I keep a pencil at my house with a white napkin taped to it. If he comes in growling and snarling, that white flag is going to be waving around some door in his line of sight. That usually breaks the tension, and pretty soon we're laughing as we talk about whatever it was that he thought was making him mad. For me, he's gotta have that ability to laugh."

* * * * * *

The way a man handles, or doesn't handle, his anger seems to be a sore point with many women. For guidance I asked:

How do you want a man to handle his anger?

I WANT HIM TO TALK IT OUT. Just don't holler at me. If he feels a need to do that, I prefer that he go away and not come back until he can act like a human being."

"I'm there to listen. I want him to lay it out on the table, so that together we can get to the root of his anger."

"I don't want him to hold his anger in, but I want no violence, such as throwing things, or pulling the phone out by its cords. That's stupid, and it threatens me. I want him to talk about it in a civilized way."

"Just don't take it out on me. If he's that angry, I want him to vent it in a constructive way ... clobber some golf or tennis balls, or jog around the block. Get it out of his system to the point that we can talk about it in a sane way."

"I want him to work it through and figure it out. I respect that."

"I don't mind him ranting and raving, but not in front of the kids. And I don't want him to get physical with another person or an animal."

"I want him to speak out about it ... not hold it in."

"It's important that he express his anger to someone he can trust. A sounding board will so often soften the problem."

"Put yourself in my shoes ... to face a six-foot, two-hundred-pound man who is violent is scary. If he's busting up the place, I could be next. I want away from him until he cools down. Then I want him to talk to me about it."

"It's healthy for a man to vent anger when he has it. I don't begrudge a man losing his temper. At the same time, I realize he is temporarily insane, so I get out of the way until he cools."

"I feel any emotion, including anger, is going to happen. Fine. It's another experience and shouldn't be stuffed down, because then it will eat you inside out and probably eat everyone else you care about. Just feel it, accept it, admit it, and then get on with solving the problem."

"Anger can be very cleansing in a relationship, if it's expressed with the attitude that *we* may have a problem, and if so, what are *we* going to do about it?"

"So often anger may be the result of a misunderstanding. So, tell me about it. Maybe we can clear the air."

"There's nothing that seems to make my husband mad, and that worries me. He may be keeping anger bottled up. I'd rather he say, 'Hey, I don't like this or that,' so that I would know what I'm dealing with."

* * * * * *

Worries. To most men, the thought of sharing them is akin to admitting a weakness, or worse, to exposing an unprotected flank to a real or imagined "enemy." To find out how women felt about a man and his worries, I asked:

If a man is open with you about his worries, is he weak or strong in your eyes?

NINETY-EIGHT PERCENT of the women considered a man as strong if he was open about his worries. Comments were:

"If he said he didn't worry about anything in today's hectic life, I'd suspect he was lying. It's a plus for him in my eyes if he airs his worries."

"A lot of men try to protect their women by not sharing their worries. But his suppressing worries threatens his health. Besides, a woman can tell when her man is worried. If he doesn't share the facts, she is likely to imagine something, which means she may imagine something beyond the level of the real worry. Then she may overcompensate in one area and inadvertently ignore the area needing attention. We don't want to guess … we want the facts."

"I don't want him to deny his worries, or pretend they're not there, or try to drown them in alcohol. I want him to see what has to be done and deal with it in a grown up way."

"Worry is a fallacy. I'm a reformed worrier. Friends used to tell me I worried about what I was going to worry about next. After thinking about that, I realized that worries are not reality. *Concern* is reality. To be concerned about a teenager returning home safely is normal, but to worry about going bald seems a waste of energy. I want him to share his concerns. Problems shared are divided."

"His worrying is going to affect me, whether he tells me about it or not, so I'd rather he tell me in the beginning."

"I want him to take action against his worries rather than constantly bitch. Get them resolved, and get on with life."

"I want him to share them, instead of trying to act big and tough and trying to handle them all by himself. On the other hand, I don't want a whiner who is overly bothered by little things. I want him to select honest-to-goodness, threatening things to worry about. I just don't want him so phony macho that he won't share his big worries with me."

"A guy who shares his worries is self-confident and secure in his masculinity. That makes him sexy."

"The Bible says that a fool listens to his own counsel. In other words, talk things over with someone. If he blows off steam about something at work, or whatever, then he gets feedback from me, that helps him make decisions."

"It takes more strength for him to share his worries than to try and hide them."

"The strong guys are the ones who are solving a problem they are faced with. The weak ones just whine about it."

"No man is an island. If he keeps his worries to himself, he's stupid."

"His sharing worries with me tells me he thinks I have a brain.

That makes me feel good about myself, and him. He's a winner."

"If he's telling me straight and honestly about a legitimate worry so he can get a solution, that's great. On the other hand, if he's just trying to hook me into solving his problem for him, I'm going to run like the wind."

"His worries will affect me. I want to know what he's worried about to have a chance at helping."

"If he doesn't talk about his worries, that will probably modify his behavior or personality. That may have a negative effect on our relationship. He's got to be open with his worries, because they affect my life too."

* * * * * *

Men's egos being what they are, we try to appear "strong" to a woman. Knowing now that many times male and female definitions are different, I asked:

What makes a man strong in your eyes?

"A GUY WHO IS WILLING to trust his feelings and emotions with me."

"One who isn't afraid for me to see his vulnerabilities is strong in my eyes. I see a man as weak who can't show himself. So many people who are weak inside attack others. I see such attacks as signs of weakness."

"A guy is strong who is self-assured and doesn't kiss rear ends. He's not afraid to cry. Not afraid to show his feelings. Not only will a guy like that have fewer heart attacks, he's also sexier."

The marriage counselor had this to say about what makes a man strong: "He has a sense that life works, that problems are not a reason to give up but rather a reason to get innovative and creative about solutions. Blair Justice, a psychologist at the University of Texas medical school in Galveston, did a study about stress. He found that stress boiled down to three areas: 1) a person who sees choices has less stress; 2) a person who views obstacles as challenges and opportunities for growth, rather than as a defeat, has less stress; 3) and a person who has a commitment to someone other than themselves, such as family, or God, or whatever, has less stress. People with these three outlooks had fewer drinking problems, sleep disturbances, and relationship disabilities or other disruptive sequences in their lives. They look at stressful situations and say, 'Well, what can we do with this?' Then they roll up the dice and play the game of life. There's also a quality of strength in asking for help when needed ... seeking the expertise of a therapist, an accountant, a minister, or whatever. Strength is not necessarily doing it all by yourself. It doesn't mean you're a self-contained unit. You don't have to be a walking encyclopedia. That isn't a requirement of being a strong man."

※ ※ ※ ※ ※ ※

With so much attention being given to the effects of smoking on human health, when I asked,

Would you cut a smoker from your prospect list?

I ESTIMATED THAT AN OVERWHELMING MAJORITY of women would answer "Yes." I was wrong.

"No" said sixty-five percent of the women, which surprised me. I thought they would be so concerned for their man's health that the majority would vote the other way. I consider the figure as a tribute to a woman's ability to bend and be supportive. Apparently they want their man happy, even at the expense of shortening his life. Their comments were:

"I wouldn't cut a smoker from my prospect list, but I wish he wouldn't smoke."

"I don't smoke, but I wouldn't necessarily discard a suitor because he smoked."

"I don't have the right to tell him how to live. He knows the risks, and it's his decision."

"I would expect consideration from a smoker ... don't blow in my face or smoke when we're in enclosed areas. Even though it is a disgusting habit, I wouldn't cut a smoker from my life for that reason alone."

"People who smoke, smell. It comes out of their pores and makes them distasteful to taste. Yes, I'd cut a smoker from my prospect list. When I was younger I wouldn't have, but I sure would now."

"If he smokes and we have other things in common, I can't very well eliminate him just because he smokes."

"His not smoking would be an A-plus. That would be a positive statement about his overall character."

"You bet I'd cut a smoker from my list. I don't want somebody messing up my lungs."

"I smoke, but I hope he wouldn't." She laughed. "If I didn't smoke, I'd be so perfect no one could stand me."

"No, I wouldn't eliminate a smoker, because I allow for some imperfection. But I don't think he would tolerate me if I smoked."

"Are you saying you think females are more tolerant than males?" I asked.

"Exactly. Females are taught to be more pliant and long-suffering, where men aren't. For instance, my dad quit smoking after fifty-five years. My mother had harped about it forever. Six months after he quit, she asked him to please smoke again, because she loved him more when he was satisfied than when he was a grouch. She said she'd rather see him die earlier and happy than live longer and miserable."

"If I were considering two guys with about equal appeal, if one smoked and the other didn't, I'd go for the one who didn't."

"I advise my teenagers not to date someone they might not consider marriageable. I tell them that love can fall on a shithouse just as quickly as a mansion. In other words, if you don't want a smoker or a drinker, cut him off at the pass and get on toward someone else."

* * * * * *

What are your comments about liquor and men?

WOMAN AFTER WOMAN said, "I don't want a drunk." A few comments were:

"I'd rather have a guy who doesn't drink. Candlelight and wine is okay, or beer at a party. But I don't want to deal with hangovers all the time."

"Men are already stupid enough without having to deal with them when they are stupid drunk. I don't like their loudness, vulgarity, and the expectation that the world accept whatever they do when they're drunk. When they sober up, I hate it when they excuse their outrageous, liquor lubricated behavior with 'I didn't know what I was doing.' Bull corn. If they think they're not going to control themselves when they drink, then don't be so stupid as to drink. But there is a clue there: what they do drunk is what they'd like to do when sober. Seeing the liquored side of a man can save me a lot of wasted time on what I otherwise thought might be a prospect."

"Alcohol combined with a man frightens me."

"There's nothing better than to have a couple of drinks with an intelligent man and watch him relax ... often he becomes even more interesting. But if he isn't intelligent enough to know when to quit, I'm moving on."

"A little alcohol with a man can be delightful."

"To enjoy a drink or two is one thing, but to use it to become stupid is another."

"I don't mind liquor, and I love men. But only if they control it."

"The guys who can't handle liquor are usually, deep down, not much good."

"I can't deal with a man who can't think, and nobody thinks straight when they're bombed."

"I missed a lot of 1970 and 1971 because I was bombed on drugs and alcohol. I missed so much that I won't have anything to do with a man who wants to go through life wasted."

"It takes very little liquor to melt my inhibitions. For a woman, the mixture of men and liquor can be explosive and dangerous. A woman should consider that before she tackles liquor with a man. If she's on the prowl, she's going to get what she's looking for in a liquor/man mix. The liquor may make her feel justified in going to bed with somebody. But if she's not on the prowl and not looking to get laid, liquor and men are to be avoided."

"I enjoy a drink. But when I drink with men, it's like they're trying to outdo me. They seem to keep track of how much I've had. When I say I've had enough, they seem to have to keep drinking. I think it has to do with them trying to prove they can drink past me. At that stage, invariably a drink I haven't ordered shows up in front of me. That makes me so mad—there's no way I'm going to drink it. If they're playing a game of chicken, at that point I'll let them win ... if win is the right word ... every time."

Another woman said, "Drinks are fine. Drunks are not."

*　*　*　*　*　*

"Watch your language ... there are ladies present" was a common warning when I was growing up. Although I hear that warning less today, I thought it might be worthwhile to ask:

What are your feelings about a man and foul language?

NINETY-THREE PERCENT of the women said they disliked foul language. Their comments were: "I don't like men who resort to force, and foul language is a form of force."

"Profanity is an insult to my ears, and an indication of his level of intelligence."

"I feel sorry for the man who uses foul language. That says to me the poor guy has no other way to express himself ... same as ignorant."

"Colorful language can be interesting. Occasional use wouldn't cause me to draw a line of rejection. But I don't want that language as a life-style."

"If he can't discipline his tongue, chances are he can't discipline other segments of his life. That kind is not for me."

"If you have nothing intelligent to say, then swear or curse. So, if he hits his thumb with a hammer, he can go foul. That's why foul language was invented ... to cover those rare times when nothing can be said that makes sense."

"A man with a four-letter vocabulary has a four-letter mind."

"I see a foul mouth as driven by a mind that's shallow, overemotional, and irrational. It seems they use profanity rather then try to solve the problem."

"Those words turn me off, especially the "F" and "MF" words."

"I sure don't want foul language to be his mother tongue."

"Simple minds speak foul language."

"A foulmouthed man probably isn't the type that would be interested in a candlelight dinner."

"Either he has a limited vocabulary, or is very angry. Either way, I'm not interested."

"I'm one of the guys and their foul language doesn't bother me. However, in a business atmosphere, I prefer they have clean mouths."

"Since I've joined the work world, I just ignore it."

"I don't respect the guy with a foul mouth and find myself saying under my breath, 'Lord, forgive him.'"

"I accept it. Everybody has a right to how they communicate. Words are just words. Hearing 'fuck' doesn't bother me. However, I exercise my right not to spend time with such a man."

"Boring language equals boring man."

"I have found that people who have a nearly total foul mouth are nearly totally angry."

"Foul language spells laziness, lack of intelligence, and lack of respect. When one of the guys says 'fuck' in my presence, it's refreshing when another reminds him to watch his language. That's nice, and I appreciate it."

* * * * * *

What are your comments about religion and the man you choose?

EIGHTY-NINE PERCENT of the women said they wanted their man to have at minimum a belief in a higher being. Their comments:

"I have respect mixed with disillusionment about the church I was raised in. Today I'm not part of any organized religion, however I want a man who has some soul ... some recognition of the possibility of a higher power. At the same time, I can't handle a religious nut. I want a man who is open-minded about religion and can respect other people's need for it."

"He has to have some sort of belief. I don't want a staunch, religiously narrow-minded person. Since we don't have all of life's answers, we obviously need some outside guidance."

"If there were radically different religious beliefs, that would make it difficult raising kids."

"I want him to be God-fearing, but I sure don't want him in a cult."

"Spirituality is the issue, not religion."

"Religion is fine, but I don't want that to be the dominating force of his life."

"I want him to believe in a religion. Not because he might think I pushed him into it, but because it's important to him."

"I couldn't relate to someone religious. I'm too free thinking for that."

"He has to have faith in the Lord and be thankful for his life, including our marriage and relationship."

"I would hope he believes that there are spiritual forces that rule the universe."

"I want him religious, but not a fanatic about it. I don't want a Jesus freak where religion controls his life."

"If a man is as comfortable with his religion as he is with his favorite sport or hobby, I figure he has pretty well got it together."

For a brief period in my life I sold insurance. In the process I met a few married men who absolutely refused to insure themselves. Their wives seemed embarrassed by their husband's stand. So I asked,

What are your comments about a man's refusal to insure himself to cover your financial needs in case of his death?

EIGHTY-NINE PERCENT of the women said they didn't like the idea of their husband not insuring himself. Their comments were:

"My ex-husband had the attitude that if he left me insurance money, I would blow it with some jerk after he was gone. I thought that was an extremely selfish attitude. I was resentful, and you will notice he is 'ex.'"

"If he refused to insure himself, I would take that to mean he didn't care about me or our children. That's selfish and inconsiderate."

"I have enough education to hold a good job. If he died, I'd simply take care of myself."

"Not insuring himself would bother me. I'd want enough to cover two years worth of bills to give me time to learn to support myself."

"That would be the same as him saying he was with me strictly for what he could get out of me. If I discovered he had that attitude about insurance, I would end it as soon as I could."

"I don't believe in life insurance, so that wouldn't bother me at all."

"That's really dumb. I had a friend with a husband like that. He said why should he insure himself when he wouldn't be around to enjoy it."

"Such a man would prove he isn't a loving man."

"I'd be considering divorce if I got tricked into marrying him and found out later he felt that way about insurance."

"If he thinks I'm going to blow any insurance money he leaves, then he isn't entitled to be with me when he's alive."

"Love is eternal and should come from the grave too."

"I'd quietly take out enough insurance to at least plant him."

"I was a young widow. I'd never consider a man who didn't believe in insurance."

"If he didn't insure himself, I'd suspect he wasn't planning a long-term marriage and maybe thinking about skipping out any minute."

In "traditional" (Eastern) societies, a bride moves in with her husband's family. In the event of his death, male family members, such as brothers, uncles, and cousins, assume the responsibility of providing for her and her children as long as they live or reach maturity. Insurance is a Western society invention to serve that same purpose. Females select a man in part for his ability to generate resources that will be available at least through the years it takes to raise their children. Rather than counting on his male relatives, insurance is our women's hedge against premature loss of the man with whom she has invested her sexual strategies.

* * * * * *

Some men I know feel threatened by a single woman who has lived alone for a year or more. (Deep down, I believe there is an unspoken fear among men that they need women more than women need them). To find out why a woman preferred living single I asked:

What is, or was, at the top of your list of likes about being single?

THE MOST COMMON ANSWER I heard was, "*Freedom* to come and go and do what I want, when I want, with whom I want." A few comments were:

"Not having someone to hassle with over little shit, such as how to put the toilet paper on the roller. And when it's quiet in my house, it's neat that I don't have to worry that the silence means someone's mad over some little insignificant crap."

"Freedom. If I get a traffic ticket, I can laugh, because I can pay it and nobody's going to have a chance at criticism or snide remarks."

"I like not having to answer to anybody. Last night it was fun to go the video store and pick what I wanted. I felt so good that I almost hyperventilated. But at other times all this freedom is scary."

"As a single I'm secure in my world. Nobody comes into my

house without my permission, and I can put them out when I don't want them around."

"I can golf as long as I want or stay at the office as long as I want with no worry about supper or anything else."

"I can spend my money however I want. I love that."

"I have a love 'em and leave 'em attitude. If things happen I don't like or agree with, I kick 'em out of my life."

"I ended a relationship about a month ago. No remorse, no sadness, or feeling like a part of me was missing. I'm real happy single."

"I'm having a blast as a single. I travel, I'm wined and dined, and I'm treated like a queen."

"I enjoy being single because I'm not beat on or controlled."

"I was carefree when I was single. Worries came with marriage."

"When I'm sleepy, I have a choice: I can go to my bed, or if I'm in the mood, somebody else's."

"I like not having to stretch my life around somebody else who may not even give a shit."

"Likes about being single? There wasn't anything particularly wonderful about being single. Being able to come and go as I please I liked, but being alone wasn't that good a trade. Besides, with the man I'm married to, I pretty well come and go as I please now."

* * * * * *

What did you dislike about being single?

THE MOST COMMON ANSWER I heard alluded to *being lonely*. Other comments were:

"I miss not having a dependable companion or escort."

"I miss the sense of family."

"I miss having someone to sleep with, and someone to share the joys of good events and the weight of the bad times."

"I miss not having that one person. And that's stupid, because it says I want to have my cake and eat it too. But once in a while I need a mental pump up, and not having one person I can tap into is rough."

"I keep so busy that I try not to have time to get lonely. Every now and then, however, I do get extremely lonely."

"I feel insecure without a committed relationship ... a marriage."

"I miss not having companionship at my fingertips."

"Not having someone's mind to share, and not being able to share mine."

"Growing old alone frightens me."

"I miss what is probably just a physical animal need, and not necessarily for sex, but to be cuddled with warm arms. A vibrator can do just so much. It can't cuddle and hug and kiss."

"It frustrates me when something comes along I can't handle, such as a stubborn jar lid."

"I don't like the dating scene. It's a merry-go-round meat market."

"I don't like eating alone."

"The fear of AIDS and herpes is at the top of my list of dislikes about being single."

"I dislike the financial disadvantage."

"It's very lonely to go home at night and not share my day with somebody. That tends to induce unhappiness, because I don't have a chance to get emotions out of my system. I'd rather be married than single."

* * * * * *

What man among us hasn't wanted to impress a female so badly that we may have put on a macho act? My next question was,

How do you react to men who act macho?

THIS QUESTION DREW one of the highest agreements among the women I interviewed.

Ninety-nine percent of them said they were turned off by (phony) macho behavior. (One found it "cute.") One woman said, "We don't like those guys." Another drew a line between "phony" macho and "real" macho. Phony seems to be a total turn-off for the women, while real macho that has been fully earned and is accredited is acceptable. "But then only if he doesn't act macho."

Here are more of their comments:

"It's dishonest. It's an act to mask who they really are, and it's a fast turn-off."

"Self-confidence is a big thing with me. Acting macho is the opposite of self-confidence. I shy away because it causes me to think they are insecure."

"I think they have an inner problem."

"I'm impressed all right ... laughing inside at them."

"Quick turn-off. That first impression is the last, with no chance for another run."

"What are they trying to hide? They must be shallow if they have to be so all fired macho."

"A little macho is okay ... the self-confidence part. I don't want a wimp. At the same time I don't want a man trying to prove himself through a steroid mouth."

"A masculine man is solid and sure of himself. He knows who and what he is. Macho guys are hollow."

"A macho jerk's bucket has too many holes for me to fill."

"In grade school the boys showed off to get your attention. When adult males do that, it tells me they haven't grown up."

"So many men think macho is working out to grow these big muscles. That's not macho to me. Nor is a big mouth, or starting fights to prove their manhood, whatever that is." She laughed. "I like a man who is macho in a manly way... a gentleman who is comfortable opening doors for me, and so on."

"A man who is genuinely macho turns me on, but he doesn't act macho. He is."

"I think they may wake up some day and discover they have let a lot of life pass them by—and some good women."

"Ass holes."

"Real sexuality is subtle. Fake sexuality (macho) isn't subtle. It hits you over the head or between the eyes. That isn't pleasant to a woman."

"I laugh at them, or sing them the lines from REO Speedwagon: *She doesn't like the tough guys, their brains are where they sit. They think they're full of fire, and she thinks they're full of shit.*"

"I associate masculine with inner strength. Honest machismo doesn't suggest power ... it's a frame of mind."

The public service company spokesperson said, "A man is macho when he is gentle with a baby, or genuinely interacts with someone with whom he has nothing to gain. He's macho when he's gentle and not self-conscious and afraid of being thought a sissy, or effeminate. He's macho when he steps out of the role society commonly puts males in. For him to be gentle and tender with an animal, especially a baby animal, is macho. Or to see him gentle with a sick old lady, one who needs nurturing and has nothing to give the man in return. Things like that are pure macho with a capital "M." A man like that brings a lump in my throat, and I want to say, 'Bless your heart, I love you so much.' He puts a big, rough, puffy authoritative man in the shade."

The one lady out of one hundred who liked macho said, "I think it's an image they've created in their heads about what a man is supposed to be. It's kinda cute that they think they are so cool and tough. And the ones that act the toughest are usually the biggest teddy bears, and that's very funny."

* * * * * *

Many of us find it tempting at times to try and impress a woman by bragging. To find out how effective that strategy is, I asked:

What is your impression of men who brag a lot?

NINETY-EIGHT PERCENT of the women disliked braggarts. There comments were:

"Bragging is a clear indication of low self-esteem and low self-image. Bragging indicates he, or she, doesn't feel very good about themselves."

"It shows they are insecure and/or immature. They have an ego that needs to be boosted constantly. I don't have time for that ... bragging is a turn off."

"I'd rather see it than hear about it ... actions speak louder than words."

"Id like to stuff cotton in his mouth. I don't know what to believe and what not to believe, so I can't take him seriously."

"If he pars the course, I would rejoice in his good news. But if he tells it five times to every person we run into, that would get old."

"If they brag a lot, that's probably what they do best."

"I like a man who has a lot to brag about, but doesn't."

"The best car on the market doesn't blow its own horn."

"They're stroking themselves because they don't have anybody in their lives to give them strokes. That says something about them that worries me."

"If they truly have mastered something difficult, they may be entitled to a little bragging. In fact, what appears to be bragging may even be more sharing than bragging. So I'm careful in my judgment. I'm also quick to spot hot air."

"There's a fine line between bragging and confidence earned from doing something well."

"Hey, bragging is okay if he's done it. Will Rogers said, 'If you've done it, it ain't bragging.' I like a man who's secure enough that he can brag about an accomplishment ... in moderation. But if he's bragging about something that is fantasy, that's a different story. He's only earned bragging rights if he's done the deed."

* * * * * *

Women are sometimes referred to as "homemaker." More and more men are sharing that activity with their woman. Since men historically have less homemaking experience than women, we may improve by understanding their viewpoint. I asked the women,

What makes a home a home?

I FOUND IT INTERESTING that not once did a woman describe a home by using a physical description, such as "a brick, three-bedroom split-level." Without exception they defined a home in terms of atmosphere. Here are their comments:

"Home is where there is a union of his interests and mine in a loving, warm, caring atmosphere. I didn't have a home in my first marriage. I had a beautiful house and beautiful things. But it was never a home, because it lacked love."

"A place where you can say and do anything anytime you want and feel free and safe. Our counselor asked us that question. When my husband defined our home as 'pictures on the wall,' that was the end for me."

"If the people living together don't get along, it's not a home."

"Love makes it home. You have a better home living in a tent with warm love than a mansion with cold emotions."

"Home is an atmosphere, not a physical plant."

"In Santa Fe, people felt our home was a safe place to be, where we could be ourselves. No hype, no phony baloney, no tensions or stress. Warm, safe, and friendly, where we could be silly or stupid, or whatever. Free. Real free."

"It's a home when you *want* to spend time there with family and friends."

"I have found that it's only a house when people who live there aren't comfortable there, so they are off to the bar, or out doing other things."

"Paint is peeling in places and my kitchen cabinets are ancient, but we have the most warm, wonderful home I've ever had. Home has nothing to do with the building. My parents live in a cathedral ceiling building with upper-middle class trappings, but I didn't feel good there. It was a beautiful, expensive building, but not a home. My little 900 square feet of peeling crap is a home."

"A home is a place where you can relax and recharge for the next day's battles. A place of privacy and intimacy. An island. A safe house."

"Home is where you can feel at peace. It's a place where you don't have to put up a front to the outside world."

"Home is where you'd rather be than any place in the world."

"If people get along and things are being worked out in peaceful ways, then it's a home."

"It's where you can relax and feel as if you can take off your shoes and fart or belch ... be casual."

"Home has more relaxed rules than your workplace. If you have strict rules, such as where the toothpaste *must* be, or this door has to be shut, or open, you're in a restricted environment too similar to a workplace. Crap on that."

"Peace, love, security, honesty. The things that make a good relationship make a good home."

"I was raised poor, with few material things. But I had a loving home that had more warmth and room for personal growth than most of my friends."

"One person lives in a *house*. It takes two or more who love each other to make a warm home."

"When we married, he moved in with me in what had been my apartment. My old place didn't even seem like a home to me after he moved in and neither of us was comfortable there. We tried redecorating it, but too often we disagreed ... I was too satisfied with the way it was. So *together* we picked a different place and moved. We both contributed to decorating and furnishing it without any big problems. We're a lot happier now ... partly because it's ours."

"Home is a civilized refuge from an uncivilized world."

"I hope our friends have two definitions of where we live. First, and more important, define our home's atmosphere, and second, and less important, describe our house."

* * * * * *

How important is it that a part of your home is your space exclusively, on a scale of zero to ten?

FORTY-NINE PERCENT of the women attached a nine or ten importance to space to call their own. The average importance on a scale of zero to ten was 7.18. Their comments were:

"Ten. I need a space that is all mine, with my identity. Between work, kids, and housework, I need a little island I can retreat to and be me for me."

"I'm good at getting my own space by piling stuff on stuff. I've been told that my stuff is an amoeba that tends to grow and multiply on its own."

"If I have peace in my life, I don't need a special place that's just mine. But if peace is lacking, I really need a special space."

"The only thing I want private is my mail. If it's addressed to me, I want to open it first. After that he can read it the rest of his life if he wants."

"I see our home as ours and don't need a special corner designated as mine."

"Zero. It's *our* space."

"Everyone needs their own space, even if only to go in the bathroom, lock the door, and soak in the tub. Eight."

"Space? Just as long as he leaves my underwear drawer alone, I'm fine."

"My space exclusively? If I loved him, I could live in one common room, but if I didn't love him, a mansion wouldn't be enough space."

* * * * * *

Greta Garbo's famous line, "I vant to be alone," prompted me to ask this question:

How important is it that you occasionally have time to yourself?

EIGHTY-ONE PERCENT of the women rated the importance of occasional time to themselves as a nine or ten. The average of their responses was 9.3. Their comments were:

"When I need time alone, at that moment it's a ten. So far this year it has happened only once. We were supposed to go to a party, and I told him I really didn't want to go, that I wanted to be alone. I loved him for understanding."

"Ten. I enjoy being alone once in a while. It helps me touch ground and get things back into focus. It helps me unwind and relieve stresses that I can't necessarily talk about with someone else. I enjoy a quiet time."

"Absolutely time alone ... ten ... twenty."

"I need a time where nobody can intrude on my thoughts or use any of my energy with demands that I fulfill their needs. I have sent my husband and our daughter camping so that I have some time that is mine. It's important not only to a woman, but to a man as well."

* * * * * *

I've known males who thought that domination of a female was a sign of his love for her. My question to the women about domination was:

What are your feelings about being dominated?

NINETY-SIX PERCENT of the women said they disliked domination, while four percent said they loved it. A majority listed domination as a factor in marriages/relationships they terminated.

The TV news photographer said, "I was raised to believe you grow up, marry your high school sweetheart, have 2.3 kids, 1.5 dogs, a two-car garage, and so on. I did all that, but wasn't happy. I traced my unhappiness to his domination over me. He selected my friends, my clothes, decided how I should laugh and speak, how long I could talk on the phone, etc. At first I accepted all that as normal. Then, after about four unhappy years I said, 'Wait a minute ... I played by the rules ... why aren't I happy?' I concluded the main reason was that I had changed my opinion about being dominated. Domination robbed me of my individuality. I was simply Mrs. Blah Blah. I didn't have a name; I was just a thing, this cute robot who served meals, did laundry, and pumped out kids." She paused. "Overnight I hated it. But when I put my foot down and took charge of my life, he blew the roof. So I told him, 'To hell with this,' tucked the kids under my arm, and flew the coop."

A forty-five-year-old housewife said, "My introduction to domination came when I was about six. My father took me down to the basement. In front of a coal-fired furnace, he opened its door, shoved my head toward the heat and flames, and said I'd better always do what he said, or he'd throw me in there. Then and there I vowed never to marry a dominating man. (My dad thought he dominated me the rest of my young years. Actually, I fooled him into thinking that.) Years later a man came into my life to whom I was very attracted. He turned out to be dominating, so I politely said 'no.' He said he'd change any way I wanted him to, but I figured he'd promise anything to get me, and then after marriage do whatever he wanted. I was right. He married the school beauty queen. Two months after their vows, he impregnated another girl. I grinned, went on with life, and have been happily married for twenty-five years."

The doctor's wife said of her first, dominating husband, "He was so determined to have his way, he often resorted to violence. I wanted to kill him and still do.

"Did his domination figure in the breakup?" I asked.

"You'd better believe it. And it was a good thing we broke up, or he'd be dead by my hand.... Actually," she frowned, "that day I balked at his domination, so he knocked me around, saying he was going to hammer some sense into my head. Well, I guess he did. That night when he was asleep, I got a kitchen knife. I was trying to locate his jugular when my sister came into the bedroom, screamed, and pushed me away. And I'm not even remotely that type of person. But let me tell you this: every man who is in a relationship with a woman should understand that if he's mistreating her, it might be wise for him to sleep with one eye open."

A thirty-seven-year-old probation officer felt that, "Domination is slavery. I hated it and won't tolerate it again ... not for one second. When he was in his domineering mode, he may as well have said he didn't think I had a brain."

The accountant said, "My first husband dominated. I was seventeen and he was twenty-seven and had been to college. I thought those reasons gave him the right to dominate. To make it worse, I thought domination equalled protection, which in my young, stupid way I thought was a sure sign of love. He didn't allow me to smoke, touch liquor, or hear dirty jokes. Yet he did all of those things. But I learned from the experience. I took a less dominating man for a second husband."

Miscellaneous comments about domination:

"In a way I feared my father's domination, but in another way it gave me the feeling he could fix anything in my life. After he died I realized that I was going to have to fix difficulties in my life. That's when I began avoiding dominating people."

"So long as I feel I'm my own person, a limited amount of domination is acceptable. But if I'm pushed off my ground, I'm gone."

"I think many women keep secret the fact they are being dominated. They hope nobody notices, which magnifies the problem. Domination feeds on itself. It's a trap."

A redhead said, "It took a while for me to figure out when it was domination. Now I measure it by whether he *asks* me something, or *tells* me. For example, if he asks, 'Shall we go to so-and-so's party,' or 'What do you think about going to the lake?' we're okay. Giving me a choice isn't domination. But when he announces, 'We're going to the lake ... get ready,' that's domination. The key is: are you given a choice, or are you simply told?"

One woman pointed out that domination is most always cooperative. Another said, "Domination is one long put-down."

I've noticed that some men treat their wives, and sometimes their children, as possessions, like a car or some other piece of equipment. I also noted that many of those women seemed to grit their teeth and endure. I asked the women:

What are your comments about someone who makes you feel as if they own you?

"OWNED? Yuck. Makes my skin crawl."

"Yes ... I feel owned right now. I feel like a slave; I hate it, and I'm getting out."

"When I was younger, I thought it was okay. But I got smarter and left."

"Once a guy tries that ownership stuff on me, it's war."

Another woman said, "His trying to own me was the reason I broke it off."

"A man's attempt to own a woman isn't love, it's insecurity on his part. Who needs an insecure jerk."

"Thanks for the thought, but no thanks."

"His trying to own me was ninety-five percent of the cause for the breakup."

"He had this idea that he owned me. I didn't like it, but the straw that broke my back was when he started calling me 'wife.' 'Wife do this, or wife do that.' I told him my last name was the same as his, that my first name was Janet, and those were the only names I would answer to. Since then he has called me by name, and we get along fine."

"A guy I just broke up with tried that ownership bit. He did it gradually, making me wait longer and longer before he showed up for a date. Apparently he thought he was building control over me. He was wrong. A few days ago, near the end of a three-hour wait, I said to myself, 'Bull, this is rude and outrageous.' I wasn't home when he finally showed up. He's a discard."

"At one time I felt owned, and I took responsibility for my part in that. Now I realize that no one really has that power, unless he has a gun at your head. We allow those things ... or decide we won't allow them. The moment I decided to no longer allow being owned, it became a war I declared."

"Is ownership any way to treat someone you call your equal, loving partner? That kind of treatment doesn't make me feel equal, or put me in a loving mood."

"I was a trophy for this one guy. It was neat, until I found out that a trophy isn't allowed to talk or think. I stopped dating him."

"My second husband treated me like a thing. I was just a woman who filled his needs, needs no different than what *any* woman could have fulfilled. I was just a body, and it was the loneliest feeling I know."

The marriage counselor said, "Affluent men seem to feel this ownership attitude more than others. They feel that their money/status gives them license to make an ornament out of their significant other. On the other hand, guys who don't have much money may try to put a woman in the 'woman' box."

"Explain the woman box," I requested.

"The alternate name is Bimbo box. That's the box wherein she puts her makeup on before they get out of bed ... she wouldn't dare let him see her without her looking her Bimbo best. In a way, she's playing the thing game too. But what she will eventually come up against is, if the box gets a little worn, he'll just pitch her and get another box containing another woman. In that framework, all women must look alike as to hairdo, makeup, laughing in the right places, etc. Generally, men expect women aged eighteen to twenty-six to be in a Bimbo box, where they aren't supposed to have a thought with meaning, let alone express anger. Women in that setting tend to grow angry and mistrust men. Then the woman tends to become manipulative. When she realizes that the best way to get attention is when she's in the woman box, then she uses it because that's where she feels most powerful. In time she begins giving sex as a reward for getting her husband to do something for her. That amounts to pay for sex. From there it's a downward spiral. She becomes sexually vulnerable ... waiting to satisfy him. At that point she's allowed herself to become a full-fledged thing." Another woman said, "To treat me like a thing, or try to own me, is about as uncivil as you can get."

* * * * * *

A forty-eight-year-old friend has never married because he is "fixed in his ways" and fears that a woman would want to change him. His fear is probably shared by a lot of men. My question to the women was:

Would you marry a man with faults you expect to change later?

SEVENTY-SIX PERCENT of the women said, "No, they wouldn't try to change their man."

Fourteen percent said they had tried, but wouldn't again.

Only ten percent, mostly the younger women, said they would try to change a man.

When I discovered that ninety percent of the women wouldn't try to change a man, I relaxed several notches. The women's comments were:

"No. We all have faults. I tried that and learned they must change from within."

"When I was eighteen, you bet. But that was when I thought I could change the world."

"Yes. If I loved him enough, I probably would try to change him."

"No, because nobody's perfect. I'm not perfect, but only because I smoke. When you love another, you accept them, faults and good points both. I think that's the key to knowing if you love them and/or they love you just as you are. If he makes changes in himself later, I want him to do so solely because he wants to, not because I demand it. Same for me."

"I don't care how hard you try, you're not likely to change him." She laughed. "Bend him maybe, but change, no. And it's not right to ask him to change. You marry him for what he is. Why destroy him?"

"No. Once you start changing someone, you're changing part of what attracted you in the first place. In other words, it ain't broke, so don't fix it."

"I wouldn't even try."

"I tried to change two different husbands. Didn't work either time."

"Yes, I'd try to change him and probably regret it."

"I would hope I wouldn't be so foolish as to try and change him ... or him me."

"We are all what we are. I wouldn't tilt with that windmill."

"No, no, no. Men don't change. They bend a little, but whatever you don't like is there and likely to stay. Usually gets worse with time."

"No. No one should think they have the right to make someone over. That's playing God."

"Of course I'd work on him. I'd go at it slowly, turning the screws a little at a time ... not enough to make him rebel or be offended."

"When I was young, yes. But I've learned to appreciate each person for all that they are, so called faults and all. Besides, what I consider a fault might not be considered so by other people anyway. So don't tamper with his core ... just enjoy him."

"When we first married, he made a list of things about me that he thought would be nice if I changed. I didn't think that much about it until our first anniversary, when he gave me my report card. I said, 'Excuse me. I think we both have faults. Don't ask me to be dishonest by forcing me to be something I'm not.' That's the bottom line ... forcing someone to be something they're not can be dangerous. On top of that, if he has any values at all, he'd be the first to lose respect for you if you faked him into thinking you were something you're not. So you'd better be yourself from the start. After I put my foot down on his little list, we got along better and better. In fact, I sensed he did have more admiration for me for resisting that crap."

"When I was young and foolish I thought I could mold any

man the way I wanted him. I nearly lost my man, and he's really good, before I smartened up."

* * * * * *

If you could wave a magic wand and make one change in your man, what would you change?

"**H**AVE HIM DRINK LESS".

"I want to magic that macho crap out of him."

"I would make him younger so I could have more years with him."

"More self-control ... reduce his temper."

"That I could be number one in his life, instead of number two to his work."

"I would wand away his stubbornness."

"I would use my one wish to have him give more openly of himself."

"I'd change his attitude about life, to take more time to smell the roses. Take time to remember anniversaries. Take a vacation. I think if he had taken more time with his family instead of chasing the dollar, we would still be married."

"That it's all right to trust enough to fall head over heels in love with a woman"

"He's already good at working on reducing the level of his weaknesses. It took me a long time to find him, and there isn't a thing I'd change."

"I would give him the confidence to tell me if a gorgeous blonde was making eyes at him so he bought her a drink, and then came home to me."

"I'd want him to put the lid down on the toilet, or to put the toilet paper going the right way, or put the lid on the toothpaste ... little things."

"I'd cut his domineering attitude."

"I'd give him the ability to communicate better."

"I'd have him not try so desperately to please his mother."

"I would have him accept my independent spirit."

"I would increase his self-confidence, which would cure many other problems."

"To be more spontaneous."

"I'd wave my magic wand and say, 'Be more sensitive.'"

"I'd like for him not to always criticize me."

"I'd wish him into slightly better health."

"I'd like him to be more of a partner, with more involvement in decisions that affect our family."

"I would have him forget my past."

"I'd like to see him get excited about something ... climbing a tree, or whatever."

"I'd wish him out of his rut. I'd make him open to new ideas and new places and things. I don't want to be so routine. I want to be surprised."

"I would make him less materialistic."

"Give him more patience."

"I wish I could wave a magic wand and make my man feel inner strength enough to show his affection for me in public. In the store he walks far enough in front of me to make it appear we aren't together. When we eat out, he doesn't talk to me, but rather keeps looking over my head to see whoever else is there. That hurts. I want him to recognize me in public."

"Why is that important to you?" I asked.

"Because then I know his affection for me is real. The only other time he shows affection is when he wants sex. That leads me to believe he doesn't care about me ... only himself. He just has me to use. But if he'd announce to the world that hey, I love this woman and I'm proud to be with her, then it's real. Otherwise he's telling the world that look, I can ignore this good-looking woman, and she takes it because I'm such a he-man. Not in my eyes."

"I wish he would worry less."

"I wish he hadn't taken early retirement. He was so happy working."

"I would like to see him be more willing to grow ... getting better, and learning new things every day. Good changes will come out of growth."

"I want more hugging before sex, during, and after. Especially after."

"If I had a magic wand to wave, I'd make his working environment more pleasant. He loves his job, but hates the workplace he's in."

"I'd change his way of supposedly telling me he loves me. I'd prefer he showed me he loves me with true companionship. Actions speak louder than words."

"I would make him straight sexually." "He has some bitterness in him ... I'd like to change that."

"I'd make him independently wealthy so we could travel more."

"I love him just the way he is. I know his faults, and it would scare me to deal with the unknowns if I waved a magic-change wand. Thanks just the same, but I'll skip the chance."

* * * * * *

Many men spend a lot of time and treasure during courtship and in pursuit of a woman. Shooting himself in the foot is about the last thing he wants to do. To help avoid that, I asked:

What could your man do that would cause your disrespect and/or disappointment?

SIXTY-SIX PERCENT of the women answered that for their man to lie, cheat, or otherwise be dishonest would cause disrespect and/or disappointment. (Also see page 22.)

Nineteen percent answered unfaithful or sexually immoral.

Five percent said to be put down would show disrespect or be disappointing to them. Ten percent listed a variety of miscellaneous behaviors that would cause disrespect or disappointment. Some comments were:

"He loses my respect when he says he feels or believes one way, and then acts contrary to what he says. I don't want to be flimflammed."

"I hate it when he publicly exposes something very personal between us ... like my small boobs, or a private matter between us that I'm not eager to share with anyone else."

"Fidelity is important to me. And that includes more than sexual. If he isn't as open with me as he is with another female, that to me is infidelity."

"Lying is the worst. If there's somebody else he's interested in, I can handle it if he tells me up front. At least then I have an opportunity to make adjustments and maybe work it out."

"I lose respect if he does something illegal ... even it it's cheating on taxes."

"Kissing up to the boss in hopes of a promotion. That doesn't wash with me."

"I would be disappointed if he took a problem to someone

else. I think I deserve the respect of having first crack at helping him."

"For him to fool around in other women's pants would disappoint me more than anything else."

* * * * * *

To have a smooth running relationship is probably the dream of most of us. But try as we may, occasionally we get crossways with our woman. Sometimes we wonder, "What happened?" In search of some magic answer to "what happened" I asked:

What is guaranteed to trigger resentment or a fight between you and your man?

CRITICISM BY A MAN was the magic answer to "what irritates a woman most." Kinds of criticism I found on the women's Top Ten list and other nettlesome irritants you might want to avoid are given below.

"Criticism will get him an instant argument."

"If he accuses me of some crime and then doesn't listen to my side, makes a wildcat out of me."

"When he scoffs, 'that's just like a woman,' that makes me fighting mad. His implied message is that women are less than men, and I resent his implication."

"You want an argument? Picture this: I come home from work and haven't even put my purse down. Ask me, 'What's for supper, and when's it going to be ready?' I take that as criticism, and you'll get an instant, blazing argument."

"Trigger a fight? Lots of things. Statements that put me down. Making fun of me in public. His not listening. His disregard for my feelings. His ignoring me. We fight a lot."

"I get in a fighting frame of mind when he puts me down, or when he doesn't give me credit when I'm contributing to a joint operation."

One woman summed up the perils of criticism with a quote from the Indian holy man, Sri Sathya Sai Baba: "If your foot slips, you earn a fracture. If your tongue slips, you fracture someone's joy or faith … a fracture that can never be set right. That wound will forever fester. Therefore, use the tongue with care. It has extra power that can harm and hurt. The softer you talk, the sweeter you talk, the better for you and the world." Dr. Gottman claims a relationship's end starts with criticism.

"When he comes home drunk, there's going to be a fight."

"When he tells me what I'm thinking sets me off."

"Not listening to me, or interrupting, will trigger a fight."

"We argue about money, but my argument is simple: mine is mine; his is mine; and ours is mine."

"If he lies to me, I'm going to be in his face."

"Putting me down will get an argument. May I say something about put downs?"

"Please do."

"There is a difference between being put down in public, and being put down in private. In public, he may be grandstanding, trying to make himself look bigger in other people's eyes, at my expense. If it slants toward being a humorous put down, I grin and put up with it. On the other hand, a put down when we're alone is serious. He really means those kind."

The contractor's widow said, of arguments, "In our first fifteen years I fought with him on some pretty stupid issues. Then I decided 'who cares,' and got on with the more important business of living each day to its fullest. But what really brought me around to dealing with so-called arguments was when he was put on kidney dialysis. With that medical event, which is a horror story in itself, sex went out the window. One evening after his battle with that machine we were on the back patio, and he said, 'I want you to file for a divorce.' Stunned, I asked why. He said, 'You're young, and I know how loving and passionate you are in bed. It is asking too much of you to give that up on my account.' Well, his offering that to me was a beautiful display of love and understanding. I nearly exploded with pride in him, and loved him even more. What he did is what a relationship is about. His telling me that made me so strong, I was able to endure anything for him. A year after that, he died." She paused a moment. "That is my answer to your question about arguments."

The thirty-year-old quality control clerk said, "Constant arguments with my first husband made me decide I'd never marry again. Well, I met a guy. I made it clear to him that I would never marry. My resolve really put him through hell. Nevertheless, he said he loved me, wasn't going anywhere, and if I wanted to test him, have at it. He passed my tests. Even though we have different ideas on a lot of things, I eventually married him. But the difference with us is, rather than argue, we work things out in a civil manner. Both of us seem to agree that marriage has to be worked at, like working at your bowling or golf game. When there are two sides, each must be willing to *listen*, and consider the other person's viewpoint. I think more women realize that than men. Discussion ... *civilized* discussion, rather than argument, is the key."

Applying that answer to a relationship is probably equal to a few hundred dollars of professional counseling.

* * * * * *

After I finished this survey I felt that there were three key questions that revealed a lot about what was behind the makeup and mascara of an individual woman. In my opinion, her answers to the following question revealed more than any other (see pages 133 and 183 for other key questions). The question was:

How late is tardy for an appointment or date with you? What is your most probable reaction when your date finally arrives, late?

THE SECOND PART OF THE QUESTION is the important part. If her first impulse is to find out why you were late, and then react, she is probably a compatible, harmonious person. On the other hand, if she is mad as hell simply because you're late without knowing why, that indicates she tends to make up her mind without gathering facts. If you are a logically thinking man, such a woman may be difficult to live with. The reason is simple.

Assume you were late because you stopped to rescue a two-year-old from the snapping, snarling jaws of a rabid pit bull. Although she doesn't know why, that in effect is the reason she is mad at you. Further, let's presume that when you arrive, your clothing is torn and bloody. Chances are, this type of person is so mad, she may not see your wounds or notice your condition. Chances are her arms will be crossed, the toes of one foot will be tapping, and she will be scowling through you. Finding facts isn't likely to be foremost in her mind.

A second clue to the personality of a person who doesn't know why you're late and is mad anyway is that she may be overly self-centered. Such a woman may demand large amounts of your time and attention. One more comment: from interviewing these women, I discovered females to be very forgiving people, more so than males. However, on the issue of meeting them on time, being late triggered something that caused some females to toss much of their forgiving nature out the window. Here are some answers the women gave. See what you can discern about each individual woman's mental make up.

"I've had it at twenty minutes. I'm nervous, anxious, and furious. What if I'm being stood up? I can't believe I've gone to all the trouble of dressing and making up and now I'm being stood up. I should have known better than to give him a date. I get almost sick to my tummy. When he shows I'm happy to see him, but as we head out, I'll sarcastically remind him that he's late."

"Thirty minutes and I go ahead and get on alone with whatever we were going to do. If I have the tickets in my purse, I may call someone else and see if they'd like to go where we were going. In other words, I make new plans."

"Ten minutes irritates. I'm going to assume something came up that was out of his control and is causing him to be late. But if it's someone I know well and he has a tardy reputation, then he isn't tardy until twenty minutes. My reaction when he arrives is to appraise the originality of what is probably another fictional excuse."

"Thirty minutes. By that time I'm thinking he might have stood me up."

"An hour." She laughed. "I'm usually not ready until after date time, so if I have to wait for him, it's no big deal. But if I'm really expecting to be somewhere on time, I might be a little mad. Or if timing for the event is crucial and he hasn't arrived, I might be mad. But if we're just going out for a couple of drinks, I'm not all that concerned.

"He's late if he's one minute tardy. At two minutes I rate him as very inconsiderate."

"After thirty minutes, you're late. If it's longer than thirty minutes I would assume he's caught in traffic, or otherwise delayed. If he doesn't call, I would think he regarded our appointment as not very important."

"I want him on time. Fifteen minutes is no big deal for an informal meeting. Otherwise I want him right on time. While waiting, I wonder where he is, and think the least he could do is call."

"When I find a man habitually thirty to forty minutes late, I don't wait. When I was younger, I had anxiety attacks, scared he wasn't going to show up. It made me angry to think that he was being late just to jerk me around or play games with me. Now I'm a little more relaxed and feel he probably has a good reason."

"Twenty minutes is tardy. But I'm sympathetic because I'm habitually late. When my day starts at nine in the morning, if I start running late, by five o'clock my schedule is clear off, and I'm going to be late."

"If we're going to the fair or something like that, fifteen minutes ... maybe thirty is no big deal. But if we're to make a movie, or meet a lawyer, I want promptness. When he shows, I'm irritated. But I won't say much because I don't want to fight."

"After fifteen minutes, I'm gone ... good-bye."

"If I agreed to meet him at eight o'clock, anything after that is tardy. My reaction when he arrives is not to react. I wait for him to tell me why he was late."

"Fifteen minutes and he's tardy. At twenty my blood is boiling."

"I'd give him half an hour. My reaction when he shows is where was he, and why?"

"After fifteen minutes, it's insulting and shows a lack of respect."

"After ten minutes I begin to think I'm not as important to him as I thought."

"After thirty minutes I wonder if I made a mistake and got the wrong time or day, or maybe something has happened to him. I don't get upset, because there's usually a reason when a man is late."

"I'm almost always ten minutes early. When he's late, I worry that he may be lying in a ditch somewhere. That's exactly what I think."

"After fifteen minutes I begin to imagine bad things, like he might have been in a wreck, or got car-jacked ... on and on. When he shows, I'm just relieved."

"After fifteen minutes I worry that I may be stood up and I'm ready to leave. Then I consider that he may have had to stop for gas, or something like that, and I calm down."

"If he's early, I know he's interested. If he's on time, I don't think anything. If he's late, I know I'm wasting my time because he's no longer worth mine, because obviously he doesn't think I'm that important. After about five or ten minutes, I start getting angry and wonder where the ass hole is. Then I correct myself and remind myself he may have a good reason and deserves consideration in that regard. I'll keep myself in that state until he hits the door.

Then I want a reason *immediately*. If he was late for good cause, no problem. But if he was late for some frivolous reason, I'll break that date and show him the door."

"Fifteen minutes, and he'd better have a damned good excuse, signed by his parents or a doctor."

"Sometimes I've been so hard up for a date that if he shows up that day, I'm happy.

"A girlfriend's experience caused me to mellow on the issue of my man being late. One Saturday I was with her when he and a friend were supposed to meet us for a movie. The appointed time came and went, and my girlfriend became a pacing bitch. The later it got, the more she fumed about 'teaching him to show me some respect.' After an hour or so we learned that on their way to us, both boys had been killed in a wreck."

* * * * * *

Which is more important to you, a man's formal education or his intelligence?

NINETY-SIX PERCENT of the women rated a man's intelligence more important than the extent of his formal education. (Teenagers almost unanimously voted the opposite, rating his formal education as the most important.) Comments were:

"His intelligence is more important to me because that is what he was born with. Book learning can be forgotten. But if he's intelligent, he'll always have the ability to learn and grow smarter."

"I vote fifty-fifty for intelligence and formal education. I've known intelligent guys with no formal education, and I liked them. However, they had rough edges that a formal education would probably have polished."

"Both are important to me, but his intelligence is more important. Formal education can be had by anyone with the time and money ... you don't have to be intelligent to be formally educated. I've known some real geeks from Harvard and Yale."

"One of my favorite people in the whole world is Abe Lincoln. Abe had no formal education, but he was an intelligent man. However, I think education may make a difference in how a man functions and feels about himself socially or emotionally."

"I've known men with high school educations who were more

interesting humans than my medical doctor brother-in-law. I'm more interested in an intelligent man who is plowing and fertilizing his mind. Formal education is a plus, but I want a man who keeps his curiosity and keeps growing past any formal education he has."

"As long as he's intelligent enough to learn from life every day, I'm happy."

"I've been distressed by formally educated folk who can't function outside their field. I find them not worth the bother, whereas people who are attending the school of hard knocks generally have all the smarts needed."

"I want him intelligent enough to use his mind, and not just lay around and drink beer."

"I want the results of an education, and I don't care how he gets it."

"I think people can learn as much from life as they can from college."

"If he's going to be the breadwinner and I'm the homemaker, I want him to be formally educated, purely from a money-making standpoint."

"I want him intelligent. I've known too many dummies with degrees."

"He can have a formal education and not have the sense of a head of lettuce."

"A formal education doesn't mean you have brains. Look at the number of college graduates who can't read or write. If a man is intelligent, he can figure out anything."

"I've seen so-called intelligent guys do dumb things. If he's so intelligent, how come he does dumb things? I'd go with formal education. You learn things from formal education that natural intelligence doesn't give you. You also learn discipline in a formal education setting."

"I want my man to have it all ... book smarts, street smarts, and people smarts."

"Any bozo can get through college ... professors can bought and/or seduced. I want an intelligent man, so that I don't have to translate my thoughts for him to understand."

"When I'm sixty-five, I want the one with formal education, because through his working life he is more marketable. In other words, at that age give me a doctor or lawyer who has travel money stashed. But right now, at forty-five, I'll take the intelligent guy, because he'll probably be more interesting to spend an evening with."

"An intelligent man is either going to be *more* sensitive, or totally insensitive. And it doesn't take me long to figure out where he stands in that department."

"For me, no intelligence equals no relationship, but rather just existing as nothing more than a couple of warm bodies. I can do that, but be advised it will be temporary, and will end at my convenience."

"If he's intelligent you're going to get better conversation. And that's what it's all about. I don't care how good looking he is, or how tight his buns are."

"Please Lord, just give me an intelligent man ... I don't care what he looks like.

* * * * * *

What is the age of the man you want relative to your age?

SIXTY-SIX PERCENT of the women said they preferred men the same age or older. Twenty-seven percent said a man's age made no difference to them. Seven percent preferred younger men. (This group tended to be women over fifty).

The forty-five year old dress shop owner said, "I tend to be attracted to men who are older than me, but I'd dearly love to have a man who is about five years younger."

The motel night clerk said, "His age makes little difference. But if you look around, you'll find women in my age group ... twenty-nine to forty-three ... with men much younger, or much older. The reason is that so many of 'our' men were lost in Vietnam. Those age differences are socially acceptable because of that war."

Other comments were:

"When I was younger, I didn't want younger men. But now that I'm older I compare my stamina versus a man's, and a little younger than me is appealing."

"I'm forty-nine, and I wish these twenty-two-year-old boys I'm having so much fun with were older. Most guys my age just don't have the energy I have. If a twenty-two-year-old is man enough to handle me, that's fine. On the other hand, if the person were eighty and had the kind of energy I enjoy, that would be fine too. So I guess his age is less of a factor than his energy level."

"I'm twenty-six and a lot more mature than guys my age, so I don't even bother with those boys."

"I'm forty-three and I want him older, by at least ten years. By then most men have learned about life and women. They don't push us. And they don't ask for a lot of housekeeping and that kind of thing. They simply enjoy the companionship we have to offer. I like that."

"I'll want somebody who is young at heart. Somebody who can go skiing, hiking, and golfing. Even if he's a lot older."

"I'm twenty-eight and prefer younger men, but I'd be much better off with a man three years older than me."

"I don't have the self-confidence to be with a younger man. I want him my age or older."

"When I was younger I liked 'em older. Now that I'm older, I like 'em younger."

"His age isn't important ... older ... same ... younger ... as long as everything else is in place."

* * * * * *

Since I stand only five feet three inches, you may understand why I asked,

Do you want a man taller or shorter than you? How much taller or shorter?

SIXTY-EIGHT PERCENT said they wanted a man either the same height or taller. Twenty-six percent said a man's height made no difference to them, while six percent preferred men who were shorter. Comments were:

"Hugging and dancing are more fun with a man my size."

"I like men a foot or more taller than me. Someone I can look up to, and he can look down at me ... but not in a dominating way."

"Physical stature isn't important. What's more important is the person's self-assurance."

"Some six-foot men I've known were awfully short, and some five-foot men were very tall in my eyes. Depends on what they're made of."

"I want a man taller by a couple of inches so I can wear heels."

"If I'm comfortable with him, his height is unimportant."

* * * * * *

I'm sure that at one time or another most men have considered cultivating a crop of facial hair. And most men have probably wondered how women feel about a beard, mustache, and hairy chests. My question was as follows:

What do you think about a mustache? Like, dislike, makes no difference. Beard? Like, dislike, makes no difference.

Mustache:
    Like, 37%
    Dislike, 13%
    Makes no difference, 50%

Beard:
    Like, 29%
    Dislike, 25%
    Makes no difference, 46%

Hairy chest:
    Like, 36%
    Dislike, 15%.
    Makes no difference, 49%.

Random comments:

"I'd love to see what a bearded man looks like under all that hair."

"I love a mustache, but I don't like to kiss it."

"I won't reject a man because he hasn't a hairy chest, so long as his head is on straight." "Too hairy and I'll be gone."

"I dislike a hairy chest because it messes up the bathtub." "Hairy chests itch if you want to get your face there. Otherwise it's unimportant. At the same time I don't want to look at his chest hair with his shirt unbuttoned."

"Mustaches, beards, and/or hairy chests aren't turning points for me."

"If his eyes are okay, his hairy chest is okay. If they're not, neither is his hairy chest."

"I'm not going to make a marriage decision on chest hair."

"I think a mustache is sexy to look at, but I don't want to kiss it. They're like a painting ... I may admire it but I don't want it hanging in my house.

"Some men hide behind a beard. If he's not secure with himself, a beard can be a cover up."

* * * * * *

I was deep into these interviews when I got clues that caused me to wonder what was driving a few individual women. As an experiment, I added the following question to my list:

Since girlhood, have you had a life fantasy? If so, to what degree has that fantasy driven your adult life?

ONE OF THE COUNSELORS was surprised that no information she knew of existed on that concept. She mused that the psychological community might profit from addressing the idea, and felt the subject was intriguing enough to rate a study.

This is the third key question I considered important for a man to have answers to by a woman with whom he is considering a long term relationship. (See pages 133 and 175 for the other two key questions.) Determining if her adult life is driven by a girlhood fantasy provides a clue as to how married life with her might be. For example, if she is *driven* to become a ballerina, you must decide if you're willing to bend your ambitions to accommodate hers. I'm reminded of the personable, pretty, bright woman who had danced as a ballerina before she married. She said, "Ballerina dancing gave me my personality, my identity ... my very soul."

The man she married was dead set against her dance dream, favoring instead his desire that she help him become a top-notch real estate broker. She abandoned the idea of becoming a ballerina. Along the way she wanted to settle for simply dancing with him ... ballroom, country western ... anything. He refused to dance, period. Each year she hated him more and more for his stance. Eventually they divorced.

Had the gentleman known the importance of this woman's fantasy, he might have factored that into his decision about marriage to her. The moral is, if your intended is *driven* by a girlhood fantasy, her happiness will probably depend on your willingness to synchronize a chunk of your life to pursuing her dream. *Driven* is the key word. Nearly every woman said she at one time held a fantasy about how she wanted her life to unfold. However, in most cases, those fantasies sank when the woman ran aground on life's reefs of reality. With those sinkings, these women redrew their dream maps, and either let go of the fantasy or modified it so extensively that it no longer drove their lives. A few comments the women made on girlhood fantasies were:

The thirty-seven-year-old housewife said, "My girlhood fantasy was to get a law degree, marry a classmate, and live in a big house with a white picket fence, kids, and a dog. Well, my attorney-to-be classmate went to Vietnam. That squelched his, and our, dreams. When he came back he no longer believed in our country or himself. His outlook had changed drastically, but mine hadn't. So I found myself in a position where I couldn't carry out my dreams and my goals. It was so important that I be able to shoot for those goals, I ended the relationship. There's no guarantee I'll achieve my dreams, but someday I'm still going to have a shot at it, with or without a guy."

The forty-five-year-old teacher admitted, "My teenage fantasy was marry a handsome knight. I even worked in a hospital in hopes of meeting him there."

"To what degree do you think you carried your teenage fantasy into your adult life and marriage?" I inquired.

"Heavily. And when my fantasy wasn't fulfilled, the marriage ended."

"What percentage would you assign your unrealized fantasy as a cause of that breakup?"

"About seventy percent. Since then I've modified that fantasy closer to the real world."

A thirty-five-year-old secretary said, "'My girlhood fantasy was to become a teacher. That still drives my life. He was against it, so I divorced him. Now I'm raising our three kids by myself and at night and on weekends I'm going to school to get my degree and teaching certificate."

"How much influence was your pursuing your goal a factor in the breakup?"

"Big factor. The real world of the work involved in getting my degree was too much for him. I don't think he heard me before we got married, because I was open about what I wanted. He didn't understand that for me personally not to be going somewhere was not my way of life. Maybe my friends who abandoned their fantasy gave it up for something better. I don't know. They adapted where I haven't. I'm going for my dreams. But I'll say this, it's easier when someone stands behind you."

The forty-nine-year-old services manager in a defense plant said, "My fantasy was a husband, me, and our children living in a house behind a white picket fence. It drove me, and my not realizing that fantasy wreaked havoc on our marriage, which ended on that note."

The forty-year-old convenience store night manager said, "I've learned that if I fantasize a situation, too often reality is a big disappointment. So now I push fantasy into the background and plan and hope instead."

The thirty-four-year-old doctor's wife said, "I had a girlhood fantasy of being a ballerina until an auto accident messed up my knees. It doesn't drive my life now. After the accident, my mother said there are several elements that make up being a wife and mother: you have to be a chef in the kitchen, a nun in public, a whore in bed, and a chameleon the rest of the time, so you can adapt to whatever the world pitches at you. Now I have accepted the real world in place of the fantasy I had."

The twenty-nine-year-old nail salon employee said, "My fantasy was born when I was in sixth grade. All-American family with a nice husband, a couple of kids. Get up in the morning in a beautiful house with a huge kitchen and fix my family's breakfast and do all those things that only ten women could do. Go off to work, come home and take care of my family, and then go out on the town. That dream drives my life today."

The twenty-year-old cosmetologist said, "'When I was little I wanted my future husband to be older, a lot taller, and real strong, where he made most of the decisions and took care of me. Beautiful home with everything I needed." She laughed. "I've become a realist and practical. Except for the memory, that fantasy has ended."

The forty-four-year-old ad agency owner said, "I wanted to be a princess. Marry a prince and dance the night away like Cinderella."

"How much of your life has been driven by that fantasy?" I asked.

"None."

The twenty-nine-year-old paralegal said, "I wanted to be a successful career girl, one of whom everyone asked questions and opinions ... one where men depended on me. I wanted a dominant role in an important career."

"How much of your life has been driven by that fantasy?"
"Almost all of it."

* * * * * *

From chatting with these one hundred women it was obvious their relationships with men hadn't all been perfect. Many had been "thumped on," raped, put down, and so on. I wondered how they felt about men after so many had treated them less than kindly. This question turned out to reveal another facet of a woman's make up ... a facet I found remarkable.

Looking back on all of your life's worth of experiences with men up to now, has the total of their influence on your life been a plus or a minus? Give examples of each.

EIGHTY-ONE PERCENT said men had been a plus in their lives. Fifteen percent said men had been a minus in their lives. Four percent said men had been about equal in a plus or minus to them.

In my view, their answers to this question reveal much about the core of women, and what makes women tick. Here are their comments:

"A little of both plus and minus. Emotionally and how to deal with a relationship has been a minus. At the same time, from the bad deals, I learned how to gather strength and go on, and that has been a real plus. Had I not had the negatives, I wouldn't know something was shitty when I saw it."

"My experiences with men have been for the most part negative, but they turned out to be growing experiences. In fact, the negatives offered more learning opportunities than the positives."

A lady lawyer said, "A plus, because men tried to keep me down. I refused and was forced to fight harder to get where I am today. That was a minus that I turned into a plus."

"Plus. I've grown from knowing men who knew exactly what they wanted, went for it, and did it. That taught and inspired. It has guided me in teaching my children how to go about reaching goals in their lives. There have been some minuses. I'm tired of men who think life is for them only, that it's a man's world."

The bank executive secretary said, "I was married to a guy who put me down constantly. I hated sex with him. He was a minus. In time I had an affair. The man I had the affair with showed me that sex could be good and warm and enjoyable. I felt great and began to think I wasn't such a bad person after all. That was a turning point for me, because I discovered that when I felt good about myself sexually, that reflected in a positive way on other parts of my life. My sexual awakening was a real plus for me, and I owe that to a man."

The CPA secretary said, "Overall, a minus. But his negative treatment caused me to be more sensitive, to look harder at the inside of people and find the good there, and to bend over backwards not to put anyone down. So his putting me down forced me to be a better person. Even though his treatment was painful, I learned from it."

The electronics repair person said, "Plus. Men have increased my perception of people. Men are such a different breed. They make me see things in a different light. For instance, if I talk to a girl about a situation, and then a guy about that same situation, the male gives me a viewpoint I may not have considered. Men broaden my perspective."

The doctor's wife said, "My husband beating and raping me and mentally trying to destroy me and my children was a minus. Yet, that minus was also educational, because it pointed out to me areas of vulnerability I didn't know I had. As a result I'm stronger, which is a plus. I think that although men have physical strength over women, women are more cunning, and can be more vicious. A woman is also more premeditated. A woman will lay plans for a calculated destruction, whereas most men just blow their top. A woman starts at the base level and goes up and won't stop until the individual she's after is destroyed. I don't think a man does that. A man will achieve a certain level of submission and back off, whereas a woman looks for total destruction. I think God did that because he put the children in the care of the woman. In a lion pride, it's the female who cares for the babies. She defends them and feeds not only them but the entire pride. The male is more dominant, while she is more cunning. I think God built us that way because females have to be incredibly soft for our children in their tender moments, but at the same time hard as nails to protect them. Abuse of the children is what led me to leave my ex-husband. When he beat them, something inside of me said, 'Get away.' After that, when I was single with my two kids, I figured a man was good for a dinner out, and if I was horny, a good screw. That was all I wanted. After that, go away ... you have served your purpose. I didn't want them around my kids or my house. Eventually, I remarried, and if we go as we are now for five more years, I'd give my experiences with men overall a plus."

The radio sales person said, "My first sexual experience was extremely positive. I am still in contact with him today, almost thirty years later, but not on a romantic level. I tell him the reason I think I have such a healthy attitude toward sex is that I was lucky enough to have him as my first sex partner. I've expressed gratitude and appreciation to him for how sensitive he was. For me, men have been all plus."

Other comments were:

"Even the bad relationships gave me a foundation to learn from, so even though they were negative, they were positive because they enlightened me to something. Among other things, I learned to recognize things about a man that might be minuses for me."

"Negative, smegative, who cares? It depends on how you handle situations. I've seen people, men and women, use what they've been through as a crutch by saying, 'Poor me. Look what happened to me and caused everything to go bad.' Plus, schmuss, who cares? I've seen people motivated by the bad that happened to them. Instead of 'poor me' they seem to say, 'Well, you got me this time, but it won't happen again,' and they get on with their lives. A little smarter, I might add. As far as I'm concerned, my experiences with men are all plus, or at least I'll make 'em all that way."

"Plus. Even with the relationships that were difficult, I had to find solutions, which helped me grow. I think women are better at this than men because we've historically been in the less powerful situation with men, so we've had to see things in a different, possibly better light ... to try to make good out of bad. On the other hand, men seem to have more of a win/lose mentality. However, a few men are catching on and also converting bad into good."

"Plus. For every relationship we have, good or bad, something can be learned from it. I can have a minus experience and turn it into a plus. My ex-husband was a minus, but he taught me that I can do whatever is necessary to survive. A plus for me."

To this I asked, "Can you think of a straight plus that you didn't have to convert?"

"Yes. Men are really very caring if you take the time to listen. Even just a date, or friend. Men care about women, a lot more than women realize."

"Even from the worst men there are things to be learned. Overall, men are a plus."

Women's proclivity to pick themselves up from bad experiences is marvelous, and their ability to learn from both the bad and the good that happens to them I find admirable.

5

Miscellaneous Nuggets of Wisdom Gleaned from One Hundred Women's Minds

DURING THESE INTERVIEWS, occasionally a woman came up with what I considered to be a gem of wisdom. In my estimation, the following are the top three nuggets:

The twenty-nine-year-old paralegal volunteered this information for men: "Men are at an unfair advantage in dating because most women won't tell a man what they don't like about him. She'll mentally keep a score card of minuses, and tell her girlfriends all about the guy. But she won't tell the guy, and she won't tell him why she won't go out with him. She'll just turn him down. Women are judge and jury on a guy, and her verdict is her secret."

* * * * * *

One of the counselors said: "I think young women are better informed about how to be in a relationship than young men because women read magazines like *Seventeen* and *Teen* while young men are reading *Playboy, Penthouse,* and *Hustler.* The young women's magazines publish articles and question/answer columns that girls learn a lot from. About the only thing the young men's magazines teach is raw sex, which for a woman may be less important than genuine intimacy. As a result, most women enter relationships more knowledgeable than men about what makes it work. After marriage, females continue their education through the *Ladies Home Journal, Cosmopolitan, Lear's,* etc. So it's almost up to women to teach their men the finer nuances of what makes a successful relationship ... and I use 'teach their men' advisedly. Many men feel they get all the teaching they need from their magazines, and besides, men believe that 'if you really love me, you ought to automatically know what I need,' which to a woman is crazy. What's worse, a lot of boys become men thinking that love is a cold beer followed by sex, while his wife's idea of love is somebody who gives her care and attention. Too often the domestic scene is, she is in the bedroom making herself pretty and fluffing pillows. She thinks that by doing those things she is showing him she loves him. But during a commercial he interrupts her by hollering, 'Hey, Babe, bring me a cold one, come sit on the couch and snuggle, and after the game we'll roll in the hay.' To him that's love. Any wonder so many relationships are in trouble?"

"Is there cure?" I wondered aloud.

"Yes. Young men can learn a lot about females and relationships simply by reading their girlfriends' magazines along with their own. If they're engaged, read at least one issue of *Bride.* After marriage, men should once in a while sandwich a copy of their wife's magazine between their girlie magazines. A half-intelligent male couldn't help but become a little more aware of a woman's viewpoint on life's important issues. If he's halfway sensitive, reading her magazine should translate into smoother sailing through life with his wife."

* * * * * *

The forty-two-year-old owner of a women's clothing store said, "Don't remarry sooner than two years after a divorce, because you need to go back and sort your thoughts to keep from making the same mistakes. If you wait as long as five years, you probably won't remarry. The reason is you become comfortable with yourself and your way of life. After you've carried your life into other activities to stay busy, you discover you can do so much more alone, especially if you're a painter, writer, or artist, etc. Productivity soars when you don't have a man underfoot."

* * * * * *

One woman had this posted from *A Woman's Worth* (Random House, 1993), by Marianne Williamson, on her refrigerator: "Some men know how to love a woman, and some men don't. Some men know that a light touch of the tongue, running from her toes to her ears, lingering in the softest way possible in various places in between, given often enough and sincerely enough would add immeasurably to world peace."

* * * * * *

One-on-one interviews with a hundred women taught me that most women have a nearly unlimited reservoir of receptivity, empathy, compassion, flexibility, and nurturing. I came to admire their ability to operate on a level different from the seemingly purposeful ego level common to many males. I especially respect their capacity to perceive and honor that which is not visible. I salute feminine energy. Our world is infinitely richer because of it, and so am I.

The Interview Questions
In the Order They Were Asked

THIS IS THE LIST of questions I asked the women. They are in the order asked. Eighty-two of them were selected for presentation in this work. You are welcome to use the list for evaluating a woman in whom you might be interested.

1. Why do you think many women and men don't get along smoothly all of the time? (Causes of conflict)
2. What can a man do that makes you feel good about yourself?
3. What is your idea of an enjoyable way to spend time, such as an afternoon or evening, with a man.
4. What can a man do that annoys you or makes you feel uneasy, such as on a date?
5. Who was the first male who was a positive, important influence on your life? What age were you?
6. What is the number one most important item you want from marriage or a relationship with a man?

7. What is the second most important item that you want from a man?
8. Many men might say you want money from them. How do you respond to that?
9. Who is the largest waster of money, men or women?
10. What is your opinion as to a weakness you consider common to males in general.
11. Do you envy any qualities or traits you think are common to males in general?
12. Is your closest friend male or female?
13. How important is it that your mate and you have similar interests, or even like vocations?
14. What does "being taken care of" mean to you? What does it mean to John Doe?
15. What is your definition of intimacy? What do you believe intimacy means to a man?
16. Have you ever felt you were dominated by a male? What were the circumstances? What are your feelings about domination?
17. Do you now or have you ever felt a man thought he owned you? What are your comments about feeling owned?
18. Do you feel any men in your life have considered you to be more a thing than a person? What are your feelings about that?
19. What could a man (or your man) do that would cause your disrespect and/or disappointment?
20. If you discovered your man had lied to you, what would be your reaction?
21. What is guaranteed to trigger resentment or a fight between you and your man?
22. How important is a man's social status in your dating or relationship choices? (0 to 10)
23. Which is more important to you, a man's present earning capacity or his future earning potential?

24. How important is it that you have an ongoing close friendship with a male? (0 to 10)
25. On a scale of zero to ten, how important is sex to you personally? To him? (0 to 10)
26. Describe your version of a sexy man.
27. Do want a man taller or shorter than you? How much taller or shorter?
28. If you had to give up hugging and caressing forever, or sex forever, which would you give up?
29. When you fail to have orgasm, what percentage of the problem do you assign to your partner?
30. How do you feel about a husband believing he is entitled to sex with you on demand?
31. What is your definition of a loving man?
32. How do you respond to a male who is unknown to you ogling your body? A male you are intimate with?
33. Sense of humor, how important is it in a relationship? (0 to 10)
34. Do you think some men fear women? What do you think they fear?
35. How important is it that sex is a part of your life? (0 to 10) Making love? (0 to 10)
36. Does any special physical trait turn you on when you meet a man, or see a man in the store, parking lot, office, or on a movie/TV screen? (Do you have a fixed idea of how the ideal man looks, his size, etc.?)
37. What attracts you to a man?
38. What are your feelings about a man who has *Playboy/Penthouse*/etc. at the top of his reading list?
39. How do you want your man to handle his anger?
40. If a man is open with you about his worries, is he weak or strong in your eyes?
41. What makes a man strong in your eyes?
42. In your opinion, who are more selfish, men or women?

43. Mustache: Like? Dislike? Makes no difference? Beard: Like? Dislike? Makes no difference?
44. Hairy chest: Like? Dislike? Makes no difference?
45. What are your feelings about a man and foul language?
46. In what order do you think men want the following elements from a woman?
    a. housekeeper/cook
    b. sex/making love
    c. companionship
    What order would you prefer?
47. In your experience with men, when a man says, "I love you," what does that mean to you?
48. What do you get from sex? What do you get from making love?
49. Do you have preferences as to who should initiate sex?
50. How important is orgasm? (0 to 10)
51. How important is the size of a man's penis? Do you prefer large or not so large?
52. How do you feel about giving oral sex to a man?
53. How do you feel about receiving oral sex from a man?
54. Which is more important to you, your man's formal education or his intelligence?
55. Would you prefer he have more education than you, equal, or less?
56. Should he be smarter than you, equally as smart, or you smarter than him?
57. Do you expect to work or pursue a career with marriage?
58. What percent of housework help do you want from your man, a) if you both work, b) if only he works?
59. How important is (or was) it that you, at some point in your life, have children? (0 to 10)
60. Liquor and men ... your comments.
61. Would you cut a smoker from your prospect list?
62. In your opinion, who has the most will power, men or women, say, for quitting smoking or dieting?

63. What kind of relationship would you prefer your man have with a) his mother; b) his sisters; c) his daughters; d) his ex-wife.
64. What are your feelings about other bed partners in your man's life a) before you, b) during his relationship with you.
65. At the time of your first sexual experience, for which reason did you choose to let it happen: a) romantic fulfillment, b) heat of passion, c) to deliberately lose virginity, d) curiosity, e) rape.
66. What is your level of concern about herpes? (0 to 10) AIDS? (0 to 10) other STDs? (0 to 10)
67. Would you rather your man have a job he is unhappy with that pays more, than a job he likes that pays less?
68. How do you think men feel about their woman having a job with more pay/prestige than theirs?
69. What could a man expect of you that you would dislike more than anything else?
70. How would you use a larger amount of surplus money that you and your man have left over?
71. What is the age of the man you want relative to your age?
72. How do you like your man to dress?
73. How late is tardy for an appointment with you?
74. Religion and the man you choose ... what are your comments?
75. What are your comments on a husband's refusal to insure himself to cover your needs in case of his death?
76. Manners and social skills of a man for you ... what are your comments?
77. What is your impression of men who brag a lot?
78. How important are handyman skills in a man? (0 to 10)
79. How important is it that you have a part of your home that is your space exclusively? (0 to 10)
80. How important is it that you occasionally have time to yourself? (0 to 10)

81. What makes a home a home?
82. Name three or four elements that make 1) a good marriage, 2) a good husband.
83. What can your man do, unexpectedly, that would please or pleasantly surprise you?
84. Do you generally like men or generally dislike men? Respect or disrespect?
85. Looking back on all of your experiences with men up to now, has the total of their influence on your life been a plus or a minus? Give examples of pluses and minuses.
86. Would you marry a man with faults you expect to change later?
87. If you could wave a magic wand and make one change in your man, what would you change?
88. How do you respond or react to men who act macho?
89. How do you think many men perceive women?
90. What could your husband do, or not do, that might cause you to consider a one night stand, or even an affair?
91. What advice would you give a man who wants to get acquainted with you?
92. What are turn-offs when you first meet a man and are making up your mind about him?
93. What do you hope for out of life?
94. Have you ever been divorced?
95. Who initiated your divorce?
96. What was the straw that broke the camel's back?
97. Have you been divorced more than once?
98. Were you battered as a child? as an adult?
99. Were you emotionally battered as a child? as an adult?
100. Have you ever felt emotionally starved? Under what circumstances?
101. Were you ever molested as a child? By whom?
102. Were you ever raped as a child? as an adult?
103. Were you ever raped as a wife?
104. Have you ever felt mentally abused?

105. Are you:
    Married? a) happily, b) not happily
    Separated? a) happily, b) not happily
    Widowed? a) happily, b) not happily
    Single? a) happily, b) not happily
    Engaged? a) happily, b) not happily

106. What is, or was, at the top of your list of likes about being single?
107. What tops your list of dislikes about being single?
108. What is your education? What is your husband's or boyfriend's?
109. What is your occupation? What is your husband's or boyfriend's?
110. Since girlhood, have you had a life fantasy? If so, to what degree has that fantasy driven your adult life?

Each woman's age, race, and geographical residence was recorded.

Acknowledgements

Special thanks for making this work easy to read: Corinn Codye, chief editor, Adele Thompson, Tania Ramahlo, Susan Smith, Elizabeth Bornholdt, Connie Hacker, Nancy Brace, Lynn Lazelle, and Dave Shivell for advice and editing.

www.ingramcontent.com/pod-product-compliance
Lightning Source LLC
Chambersburg PA
CBHW030232170426
43201CB00006B/197